SPIRITUAL
SURVIVAL
GUIDE

DOUBLEDAY

New York

London

Toronto

Sydney

Auckland

SPIRITUAL SURVIVAL GUIDE

How to Find God When You're Sick

✦

CHARLES SHIELDS
AND CYNTHIA FERRELL

PUBLISHED BY DOUBLEDAY
a division of Random House, Inc.
1540 Broadway, New York, New York 10036

DOUBLEDAY and the portrayal of an anchor with a dolphin are
trademarks of Doubleday, a division of Random House, Inc.

Book design by Ellen Cipriano

Library of Congress Cataloging-in-Publication Data

Shields, Charles, 1944–2000
Spiritual survival guide: how to find God when you're sick/Charles Shields and
Cynthia Ferrell.—1st ed.
p. cm.
Includes bibliographical references.
1. Sick—Prayer-books and devotions—English. 2. Spiritual exercises.
3. Shields, Charles, 1944–2000 I. Ferrell, Cynthia, 1956– II. Title.
BV4910 .S55 2001
248.8'61—dc21
00-060272

ISBN 0-385-50081-5

July 2001

First Edition

1 3 5 7 9 10 8 6 4 2

The creation of this guide would not have been possible but for the support of our families, the Bowen H. and Janice Arthur McCoy Charitable Foundation, the staff and members of Brentwood Presbyterian Church, and the friends, spiritual advisers, and physicians who listened, prayed, and pointed the way through the pain and upward to healing.

CONTENTS

PROLOGUE

∎

I am surviving, but it is without Charles.

My coauthor, the Reverend Charles Shields, adored life. He saw it as one enormous, inclusive ministry, in collaboration with a God who is the Divine Lover of us all. Charles's happiness in his calling showed. He bounced when he walked and when he talked, you were wise to watch out. The man had an extraordinary capacity to convince you that you were the beloved of God and the only possible volunteer to do any church job, all in the same breath.

And he knew how to draw a crowd. His premise of God's devotion gave rise to tantalizing sermon titles, posted on the outdoor display board each Monday: "Divine Desire," "Passion Doesn't Punch a Time Clock," "Guilt Without Sex," "Unruly Joy." Come Sunday, people poured through the doors. Add to that the way he sermonized, gleefully and with a wink, and at a time when congregations of major denominations were withering on the vine, Brentwood Presbyterian Church grew from one service to two, to three, and finally to four services each Sunday in a newly enlarged sanctuary. Week after week, Charles took that topic of God's divine love and served it with music, candles, and theology besides: Compassion over holiness, people over rules. It all came out as grace.

His attitude didn't change with the revelation of his terminal illness. For most of us, the news of advanced cancer would have sounded like the gates of life slamming shut. For Charles, however, the diagnosis was a gate swinging open to a new kind of ministry. He glimpsed a world full of people in his same state of physical and emotional pain. Instead of moaning over his own misfortune, he went on a mission on behalf of all who are seriously ill, looking to find the answers to the most basic of their shared questions: How do you survive the disease? How do you survive the treatment? How do you find the willpower to get up in the morning? Most important, how do you still love life? Throughout his search, Charles kept on preaching of a God who loves us in all of life's broken places, who suffers with us, who wants us to dance, and he would say later that when he was in the pulpit, he felt no pain.

Meanwhile, we wrote it all down, with a shared vision of creating a spiritual guidebook for people coping with catastrophic disease. Our backgrounds instantly cast us into roles. Charles supplied his theology and singular journey; I melded his personal story with journalistic breadth, exploring whether our spiritual prescription applied to others who walked that frightening road and survive still. It was a good pairing, each of us pushing the walls of our writing out to encompass areas the other originally had no intention of including. The entire experience of having to live Charles's extraordinary faith with him and try to see events through his eyes left an indelible mark on me. I was a witness to the progression of his disease, to his unfailing love of God even in the darkest of times, and to his will to maintain quality of life. I live my spirituality differently as a result.

In the midst of our writing, Charles continued to pray for clear vision, that he would be able to find and capture the means of a miracle. The prayers worked. Early on, Charles had ceased to respond to standard therapy and had been told by physicians that he would not see his daughters graduate from high school. But he refused to take the prognosis as gospel and, with his faith in God and his optimism intact, he concocted a combination of diet, medical treatment, complementary therapy, spirituality, and love. He blasted past the doctors' literal deadline and together, he and his wife Nadia saw their daughters Sarah and Elizabeth out of high school and both firmly settled into college.

Charles retired from parish ministry at age fifty-five to set up the Institute of Faith and Health, online support for those in catastrophic illness with content designed to blend medical treatment and increased spiritual strength. His preferred tagline to this newest segment of his mission was "Purveyors of Hope and Resources." Writing up his business plan, I told him "purveyors" made it sound as if he were selling fine wine, which, rather than putting him off, pleased him to no end.

Charles Shields took his last breath one evening in July. In all, he lived an extra three and a half years past his doctors' expectations. Not enough in my mind, but then again, three and a half decades would not have been too much.

He had asked if I would see him through to the end of this journey. How could I not? Yet reticent to intrude, I asked if he didn't want his death to be a family time. "Be there," he said. Our relationship by then was like that—pleases and thank-yous both omitted and assumed. "Besides," he said, "you're family."

And so the day came when my own family stuffed an overnight bag full of clothes for me and I drove over the Santa Monica Mountains and down Pacific Coast Highway to his home. His wife and daughters, as inclusive as he, wrapped their arms around me and took me in.

Those around his bedside say that he beat cancer even as he died of it. His last weeks were filled with candles, country music, stories, and people—lines of people in the bedroom, out the hallway, through the living room, and onto the porch—everyone waiting a turn to say that he had changed their lives. Those people will tell you that they feel his presence, still.

The service, which he wrote himself, was too huge to be held at Brentwood Presbyterian—too many folks flying in from across the country. So it was held in an enormous sanctuary high up on Mulholland Drive, where the view stretched from the Pacific Ocean to the San Bernardino Mountains. Charles had ordered up a Dixieland jazz band, specified the choir's praise songs, handpicked the speakers, and selected their topics. My job was to read from this manuscript: Charles's vision of life and death from the top ski run. In every part of that memorial service, he was audible, palpable, and merely invisible.

Now I am missing Charles dreadfully, of course. Down to the last, he proved to be his same playful self. In his final days, the hospice nurse turned to him and said sincerely, "I've only known you a few days and I'm crazy about you." He looked up at her and said, "I know." Surely the universe slowed for a moment when he slipped into God's arms.

Forgive me now, if I speak to my friend:

Charles, you have entrusted me with a wealth of unfinished projects. Though I cannot do what you could, I will do the best I can. We have walked the length of the psalmist's Valley of Shadows together. I have witnessed much and stumbled often, and with your family and oh, so many friends, I reluctantly hand you up to God. May God give you joy, parties, good wine, and country music, and above all, may God give you a mission. When I see you again, I want to hear the stories you will tell.

—*Cynthia Ferrell*

SPIRITUAL
SURVIVAL
GUIDE

JOURNEY

I am surviving.

I was forty-nine years old when I was diagnosed with cancer. Because of my relative youth, doctors had not looked for prostate tumors earlier. By the time I demanded a full examination, the discovery of the virulent, fast-growing cancer turned out to be rather late. Since that chilling diagnosis, life has had its terrifying times, exhausting times, times when my Christian faith appeared impotent. Yet, at the same time, the illness has brought with it so many gifts that I would not now trade away the experience even if I could.

During my crisis, though my faith is no more than ordinary, extraordinary things have happened to me. I am still alive because of talented physicians; it was God, however, through my meditations and prayers who prompted me to seek out the doctors, God who specifically prepared me for what was to come, and God who offers me the power to heal.

Why didn't God spare me the crisis to begin with? I don't know. Clearly, each person on earth faces a similar calamity sooner or later, without distinction between the "good people" and the "bad," people of faith and nonbelievers. Eventually everyone gets sick and comes eye to eye with mortality. But while Christians share crises with the rest of humanity, today I do know that believers have an advantage: The vast resources of the Christian faith provide the tools to navigate through crises, and the strength to meet illness head-on.

Beginning in the earliest days of our faith, Christian leaders handed down a spiritual survival kit, tools to help other followers of Christ not just pray in hours of desperate need, but pray and hear God's response. The tools were forms of meditation and prayer. Based in Scripture, they were designed to bring order to agitated thought and physical calm to chaos. Where crisis seemed to push spiritual peace away, these prayer systems brought back the ability to sense God's presence, and with the comfort and power of that presence, the ability to face crisis calmly and to move through it.

The oldest of the tools our Christian ancestors actually retained and adapted from their Jewish roots—an ancient method of reading the Psalms and the prophets that produced profound results impossible to ignore. The other method was developed in 1500 A.D.: a form of deep, dreamlike meditation that not only fostered peace of mind, but pushed past conscious barriers to hearing God.

That these simple spiritual exercises still exist today is a testament to how well they work. They are held dear by Christians around the world, but at the same time are not widely taught and so may be a mystery to many of us. I first stumbled across the exercises as if by accident. The older of the two I had learned of before my illness; the other, after the cancer had begun to grow but before I was aware of its presence.

It was with the luxury of a collected mind and assumed health that I originally explored these concepts, and it was during those initial meditative experiments that God set in motion the chain of events that led to my diagnosis. At that point, the tumor was revealed and the fear, rage, tests, and tears descended. It was again thanks to these tools that even in the midst of the emotional tumult I found God waiting for me, ready to still the storm in my life.

You may not have had that advantage of advance preparation, nor the luxury of exploring meditation with a peaceful mind. You do now, however, have the tools to open yourself to the presence of God, and you can trust that God is there, waiting.

Some people have asked as to which particular Christian church these historical exercises best apply. Interestingly, those asking have invariably been physically well and wondering whether the meditation guide would be appropriate for a sick friend. The question does not seem to occur to those of us who are gravely ill. When you are fighting for your life, the philosophical distinctions seem to require an overabundance of precious time.

By way of answer, however, the exercises are universally Christian. The spiritual tools are very old and are grounded in the power of simple faith rather than in a particular doctrine. Understand that faith and doctrine are not the same. Church doctrine represents an intellectual construct of one's understanding of religion; we learn it from Sunday school teachers, parents, and clergy. Your faith, on the other hand, is your private relationship with God. When threatened with illness, you react individually out of whatever faith you have.

The prayers and meditations that form the heart of this survival kit are not likely to alter your learned doctrine, but instead will bolster your private faith in the midst of frightening illness. They speak directly to the shock and confusion that propel you and those who love you away from relationship with God exactly at the time you need God most, and they offer simple ways to reconnect, deeper than ever before.

Unless otherwise noted, Scripture is quoted from *Today's English Version (TEV)*, published by the American Bible Society. You may find that a comparison between different translations will help you get the most out of your meditations. The power, after all, is not in the words, but in the relationship with the One of whom the words speak.

Along with Scripture passages and meditations presented in this guidebook, you will find stories of people who have journeyed through their own catastrophic illnesses. These true-life experiences illustrate the spiritual tools that help us navigate our way through troubled times, and thanks go out to these friends—old and new— for their candid memories, their sense of humor, and their willingness to share.

There are three ways to approach this book. The first is to simply read it for the stories; the second, to read the stories with the accompanying Scripture passages. Both ways, you will find emotional encouragement and practical suggestions.

The third approach is to read the stories and meditate on the Scripture. This offers you the greatest opportunity to open yourself to the presence of the One who created you. *Spiritual Survival Guide* is used most effectively as a workbook, so give yourself the freedom to write your thoughts on both the "Reflections" pages and the margins of the text, and underline passages that speak to you. The impact will be greatest if you use it in a comfortable place where you can be uninterrupted.

I hope you will take your time reading, savoring each line of Scripture. The passages, along with your memories and your imagination, will serve you well. If your illness makes reading and writing difficult, you can invite a trusted caregiver to join you. Your caregiver, too, will find healing here.

My coauthor is Cynthia Ferrell, a writer and a woman of deep faith. She and I have worked together professionally and as volunteers for more than a decade. She brings to this work her interviewing, writing, and editing skills, and her lifelong relationship with God. Early on, she decided for clarity's sake we must write in a single voice. That voice ended up being mine—a sacrifice on her part. Without her, these stories would not be recorded and these exercises would never have gone to print.

And they should be in print. I know firsthand the peace spiritual exercise can bring, a peace that crisis steals away. My hope is to assist in the enhancement and deepening of your relationship with the God who created you and loves you—the God who desires to come to you right now. When you again sense God's hand in bringing order to chaos, my prayers will be answered.

May God bless you on this journey.

—*Dr. Charles Shields, Pastor*

Before You Read Further

+ Put yourself into a comfortable place alone with this book.
+ Invite God to be present with you.
+ Read out loud the following "Promise from God."
+ Reread it slowly and hear the words as God's personal promise to you.
+ Spend several minutes letting the words sink into your heart.
+ Thank God for this time.

A Promise from God

Israel, the LORD who created you says,
"Do not be afraid—I will
save you.
I have called you by name—
you are mine.
When you pass through deep
waters, I will be with you;
your troubles will not
overwhelm you.
When you pass through fire, you
will not be burned;
the hard trials that come will
not hurt you.
For I am the LORD your God,
the holy God of Israel, who
saves you.
. . . you are precious
to me
. . . I love you and
give you honor.
Do not be afraid—I am with you!"

—ISAIAH 43:1–3, 5

7

1.

CHAOS AND
THE COMING GOD

Some moments in life stand out more than others. One such moment for me was a Tuesday in January. I remember the time: 3:15 P.M. I was in my office at Brentwood Presbyterian Church when a call came in. The doctor was on the line: "Tests back . . . Two of the biopsies . . . malignant." I'm sure he said more, but what I remember is "You have cancer."

Not just cancer. Advanced cancer. What followed was an avalanche: tests, confusion, doctors with different opinions, doctors with different reputations, a mass of well-meaning and sometimes bizarre advice. Bone scans, CAT scans, X rays, blood work. Crucial decisions had to be made in a screamingly short period of time. Which treatment? Which doctor? Life dissolved into chaos.

—CHARLES SHIELDS

From the beginning, God has specialized in bringing order out of chaos.

It was into the chaos Genesis calls "the deep" that God first came, creating orderliness and life. And when that newly created life brought a whole new chaos of its own, God continued to come, to men and women, in all places and in all times.

God came to bring order to the chaos in the lives of Abraham and Sarah, to Joseph, Moses, David, and the prophets. God came to Elizabeth, Mary, and Joseph in their times of need. To address the world's crisis, God came uniquely in the carpenter Jesus. God came to Peter and Paul in their struggles, to the first Christian martyrs and the early church thinkers, to Teresa of Avila, John of the Cross, Martin Luther, John Calvin. God came to Sojourner Truth, Toyohiko Kagawa, Albert Schweitzer, Martin Luther King, Jr., and Mother Teresa. From the beginning of time, to these and millions of unnamed people God has come, creating order out of chaos, meaning out of confusion, purpose out of crisis.

If you can only step outside of your moment of crisis, you will find God is with you, too. It is easy in the frenzy and rage that follow bad medical reports to forget that God has a history of coming to bring order. In the midst of your illness divine help may seem very far away, but God still comes today.

The journey toward order and new life, toward healing, begins by remembering. If we can recapture the memory of God's coming in our past, we can capture the hope that God will not abandon us now. Perhaps fittingly, it was through tragedy that God first influenced my life—a tragedy that occurred before I was born, but which has repercussions to this day. Here, briefly, is my story, in hopes that it serves as a jumping-off point for exploring the roots of your own faith.

My parents were Iowa farmers. My mother, one of seven children born at home, fully planned to follow my grandmother's childbearing example. So my mother kept up with farm duties, including climbing peach trees, until nearly full-term. But labor, never an easy process, for her proved to be a nightmare, and more than thirty frightening hours in pain were followed by a jostling twenty-eight-mile drive over gravel roads to the only hospital around. Of my mother and her tiny boy, only one survived. "They brought my baby to me in a casket," she said, "but they wouldn't let me hold him. They told me some mothers won't let go."

Inexplicably, my mother's crisis dissolved into faith, and pregnant again she prayed: "If you give us a healthy boy, I'll give him to you." I was born and so, despite the fact that my father rarely attended worship, my mother brought me to every activity the local church held. She never told me of her bargain with God—never, until I was twenty-four and already active in ministry. She finally brought it up one night around my youth group's campfire and explained her delay saying, "I was afraid people would think I was crazy." How often I have said that of my own encounters with God.

After high school, I enrolled in a Christian college, but to tell the truth, I wasn't certain why. I had no idea what I wanted to do with my life. I had thought I might make a career of music (with the accordion as my instrument), but that little college didn't even have a music program. Ninety percent of the graduates went into ministry and I certainly wasn't doing that.

During those four years, though—good and nurturing years in a multitude of ways—my knowledge of the Bible deepened. Over and over I was asked to work in churches, usually as a part-time youth minister, and always I loved it. Faith was growing in me; I had at last put out my welcome mat for God.

My growing faith did not make me immune from crisis. As in everyone's early life, mine had episodes of sickness, family deaths, and disappointments. The largest challenge to my early faith came with the failure of my first marriage. A student minister armed with an oversimplified, black-and-white faith, I legally performed weddings before I myself was old enough to legally wed. In my naïveté, I required of couples six sessions of premarital counseling, often answering questions couples didn't have and just as often providing the wrong answers. Then, with deep conviction, I would always say, "Erase the word 'divorce' from your vocabulary. Divorce does not exist as an option for Christians." After five years my own marriage ended in divorce. The events left me shaken—hurt, embarrassed, and of course feeling horribly guilty. God, I felt sure, was disappointed in me.

After the divorce, I spent years in counseling with pastors and a therapist, trying to find out what had gone wrong in my marriage. I never fully uncovered the answer, but I did discover what was to become the new foundation of my faith, the reality that would shape everything else I would do. While faith had not prevented crisis in my life, faith brought from the crisis a gift: grace—the surprise, undeserved, life-affirming gift of divine love. At twenty-six, thanks to the patient guidance of a pastor/mentor, a therapist, and repeated reflection on Scripture, I at last internalized what I for years had preached: We each are the beloved of God.

Before any of us ever knew God existed, God loved us. Before we were that twinkle in our mother's eye, we were the apple of God's eye. Henri Nouwen so eloquently wrote, "I hear at my center words that say: 'I have called you by name, from the very beginning. You are mine and I am yours. You are my Beloved, on you my favor rests. I have molded you in the depths of the earth and knitted you together in your mother's womb. I have carved you in the palms of my hands and hidden you in the shadow of my embrace. I look at you with infinite tenderness and care for you with a care more intimate than that of a mother for her child. I have counted every hair on your head and guided you at every step. Wherever you go, I go with you, and wherever you rest, I keep watch. I will give you food that will satisfy all your hunger and drink that will quench all your thirst. I will not hide my face from you. You know me as your own as I know you as my own. You belong to me. I am your father, your mother, your brother, your sister, your lover and your spouse ... wherever you are I will be. Nothing will ever separate us. We are one.' "[1]

We have a living God who loves us so intensely there is no painful experience God will not willingly take on and nothing that divine love cannot heal. Through my own grief and embarrassment I finally learned firsthand that our hope for healing is neither in our behavior nor in our belief, nor is our salvation from the church to which we belong. Our hope for our own lives, and for our future as a world, is in the surprising gift-love of grace flowing from our creator.

It is that incredibly grace-full God to whom I committed my life. It is that God who came full of grace in Jesus Christ. It is that amazingly graceful God who was and is the source of my salvation, my healing, and my hope for the future. To have found that lover of my soul meant more to me than any other thing in my life. Quite the opposite of alienating me from my faith, catastrophe served as the open door for the coming God.

Where was my faith, then, when this illness, this most frightening crisis came? I thought I'd learned my lessons well, but all my hard-won faith was overwhelmed by emotion. I wanted to remember the times God had come. I wanted to hold on to hope, but instead I got lost in the swirl of chaos.

[1] Henri J. M. Nouwen, *Life of the Beloved*. Crossroad Publishing Company, New York, 1992.

Know you are not alone in your feelings.

CRY OF DISTRESS

I cry aloud to God; I cry aloud,
and he hears me.
In times of trouble I pray to the LORD;
all night long I lift my hands in prayer,
but I cannot find comfort.
When I think of God, I sigh;
when I meditate, I feel discouraged.

He keeps me awake all night;
I am so worried that I cannot speak.
I think of days gone by and remember
years of long ago.
I spend the night in deep thought;
I meditate, and this is what I ask myself:
"Will the LORD always reject us?
Will he never again be pleased with us?

Has he stopped loving us?
Does his promise no longer stand?
Has God forgotten to be merciful?
Has anger taken the place of
his compassion?"
Then I said, "What hurts me most is this—
that God is no longer powerful."

I will remember your great deeds, LORD;
I will recall the wonders you did in the past.
I will think about all that you have done;
I will meditate on all your mighty acts.

—PSALMS 77:1–12

For the next few minutes, set aside your emotions and instead, reflect on your past. Concentrate for the moment on how God has already worked in your lifetime and let your memories become a source of gratitude. Since we are after peace of mind, it is important now to clear your personal slate. Life's disorders—"sins"—can block you from feeling present with God. Take this time to resolve any old sins and recommit yourself to God.

The guideline on the next page recommends that you conclude each meditation with the Lord's Prayer. That may sound monotonous, but the repetition allows this ancient prayer to become a template for guiding you deeper into a personalized dialogue with God. Though most of us can rattle off the words like lightning, slow down the process. Say the Lord's Prayer phrase by phrase, in time with your breathing.

Stay with this meditation and the ones that follow for as long as you feel comfortable, using the "Reflections" pages to jot down any thoughts.

REMEMBERING AND RECOMMITMENT

1. Offer this time of prayer to God and invite God to work in your thoughts and words.
2. Ask God for the ability to remember the power of the time you first knew you were a Christian.

    Remember your feelings.

    Remember what motivated you to say "yes" to God.
3. Review your life in three sections: the first third, the second third, and the most recent. Note particularly any discord or places where your life was and is out of balance and not working.
4. Ask God for the grace to recognize the discord in your life, and for the power to begin to be rid of it.
5. Now notice the people who have been influential in sharing faith with you. See all of the people and experiences you have pictured as gifts coming directly from God to you.
6. Give thanks to God for those gifts and for your faith.
7. Resolve to give yourself again to God.
8. Say the Lord's Prayer.

The Lord's Prayer is deeply personal. Here we supply one traditional translation. However, you should use whatever wording is most familiar and meaningful to you.

THE LORD'S PRAYER

Our Father which art in heaven, Hallowed be thy name.
Thy kingdom come. Thy will be done in earth, as *it is* in heaven.
Give us this day our daily bread.
And forgive us our debts, as we forgive our debtors.
And lead us not into temptation, but deliver us from evil: For thine
is the kingdom, and the power, and the glory, for ever. Amen.

—KING JAMES VERSION

Read and remember.

GOD'S COMPLETE KNOWLEDGE AND CARE

LORD, you have examined me and
you know me.
You know everything I do,
from far away you understand
all my thoughts.
You see me, whether I am working or resting,
you know all my actions.
Even before I speak,
you already know what I will say.
You are all around me on every side;
you protect me with your power.
Your knowledge of me is too deep;
it is beyond my understanding.

Where could I go to escape from you?
Where could I get away from
your presence?
If I went up to heaven, you would be there;
if I lay down in the world of the
dead, you would be there.
If I flew away beyond the east
or lived in the farthest place in the west,
you would be there to lead me,
you would be there to help me.
I could ask the darkness to hide me
or the light around me to turn into night,

but even darkness is not dark for you,
and the night is as bright as the day.
Darkness and light are the same to you.

You created every part of me;
you put me together in my mother's womb.
I praise you because you are to be feared;
all you do is strange and wonderful.
I know it with all my heart.
When my bones were being formed,
carefully put together in my
mother's womb,
when I was growing there in secret,
you knew that I was there—
you saw me before I was born.
The days allotted to me
had all been recorded in your book,
before any of them ever began.
O God, how difficult I find your thoughts;
how many of them there are!
If I counted them, they would be
more than the grains of sand.
When I awake, I am still with you.

—PSALMS 139:1–18

Read, and let the psalmist's desire become yours.

OUR DESIRE

O God, you are my God, and I long for you.
My whole being desires you;
like a dry, worn-out, and
waterless land,
my soul is thirsty for you.
Let me see you in the sanctuary;
let me see how mighty and
glorious you are.
Your constant love is better than
life itself,
and so I will praise you.
I will give you thanks as long as I live;
I will raise my hands to you in
prayer.
My soul will feast and be satisfied,
and I will sing glad songs of
praise to you.

—PSALMS 63:1–5

2.

FAITH IN CRISIS

■

How much longer will you forget me, LORD?
Forever?

—PSALMS 13:1

Most people assume that an unshakable faith comes in the lining of a pastor's robe. I only wish it were so. I have never felt so desolate as I have in this health crisis. Eventually, my faith did turn out to be critically important in my struggles with cancer, yet throughout much of my ordeal, it felt frustratingly impotent. Now through the initial crisis, I can look back and see God was at work, but during the process, to be quite honest, I wasn't so sure. I needed to hear from God. On the other hand, I had never been taught how to listen for God's words and tended to discount those people who said they did. So it was floundering in uncertainty that I set out to find God.

I did have an advantage. During those days when I assumed I

was well, I had explored two of the ancient tools of our religion—tools for receptivity that I, for all my religious education, had never learned before. Unlike any worship experience I have ever known, these practices taught me not just to talk to God, but to listen.

The first technique was listening for personal messages through Scripture—a logical, nonthreatening place to start, since our tradition already holds that the Bible is the word of God. In my early Christian training I had of course learned how to study Scripture. I had mastered the art of biblical literary criticism, I had memorized outlines of New Testament books and passages, some long, some short. I had studied Greek and I knew how to use commentaries, Bible dictionaries, and concordances. I was truly a student of the Bible. What I somehow missed was the art of reading the Bible prayerfully.

Then, years into my professional life, I found myself at San Francisco Theological Seminary for a Companions on the Inner Way conference led by Morton Kelsey. The conference introduced me to "Divine Reading" and I discovered that all those Scripture passages I had dutifully memorized in school actually provided a channel through which God could speak to me personally. Having now incorporated this spiritual exercise into worship services, retreats, Bible studies, and conferences, I know there is a world of difference between studying the word of God and prayerfully listening to it.

Divine Reading is a slow, thought-filled praying of Scripture, which enables the Bible to bring you into union with God. It is, simply stated, repetitive reading, out loud, of a particular passage. Each time you read, certain words will stand out as more important than the rest. These words, which often change with each reading, serve as the launching point for personal exploration and meditation.

Formally termed *lectio divina*, Divine Reading predates Christianity, with origins that can be traced to contemplative Jews who chose to live in religious seclusion outside city walls. Philo of Alexandria, the great Jewish philosopher who lived from approximately 20 B.C. to

50 A.D., recorded his observations of this ancient contemplative life, noting the enclaves' unadorned lifestyle and the inhabitants' utter devotion to God.

For six days of each week, the solemn participants sequestered themselves in sacred chambers, taking with them no food or drink, only the Psalms and the laws and oracles of the prophets. The whole of their day was given over to spiritual exercise. In accordance with ancestral practice, they read the Holy Scriptures as allegory, believing that the words of the literal text were divine symbols, to be revealed through exploration of underlying meanings. As Philo described the process, ". . . the polished glass of the words unfolds and reveals the symbols and brings forth the thoughts bared into the light for those who are able by a slight jog of their memory to view the invisible through the visible."[1]

On the seventh day of each week a banquet was held, where the eldest would select a Scripture passage for close examination and, "through constant recapitulation," imprint the thoughts imbedded in the passage on the minds of his listeners. For these people, Scripture resembled a living being with literal commandments for the human body and an invisible meaning for the soul.

Divine Reading proved so effective that it was quickly adopted by the fledgling Christian religion. The early Christian mystic Cyprian of Carthage (d. 258) wrote of steady reading and prayer which opened up glorious, personal, two-way communication with God: "Be constant as well in prayer as in reading; now speak with God, now let God speak with you . . . Whom he has made rich, none shall make poor; for, in fact, there can be no poverty to him whose breast has once been supplied with heavenly food."[2]

The practice of Divine Reading continued to be handed down

---

[1] *Philo of Alexandria: The Contemplative Life. Giants and Selections*, translated by David Winston. Paulist Press, Mahwah, NJ, 1981.

[2] From the Letter to Donatus, *The Ante-Nicene Fathers*, translated by E. Wallis. Eerdmans Publishing Co., Grand Rapids, MI, 1975.

through generations and eventually caught the attention of a disillusioned fifth-century Italian monk named Benedict. His affinity for Divine Reading was triggered by illness—not a personal ailment but the illness of society at the time.

Benedict was born in a mountain town in central Italy at the end of the fifth century when the Roman Empire was in rapid decline. He turned to the church to serve God and forsake the turmoil, only to find the church itself was morally and spiritually sick, wounded by internal schisms that had resulted in violent and bloody fighting between opposing Christian forces. Afraid for his soul if he continued in that religious hierarchy, he fled the formal training of the church, and joined a small community of monks in a small village some forty miles from Rome.

Yet even the Western monastic movement, begun centuries before Benedict was born, had weakened considerably through gross excesses and general laxity. After much trial and error, surviving assassination attempts by other monks and times of living in total solitude, Benedict embraced *lectio divina*, a practice he called "listening with the ear of the heart," as a means of discovering the underlying spiritual rhythm of daily life.[3]

His example of sheer discipline, combined with this form of deep spiritual nurture, served as inspiration for others in his own lifetime and through centuries to come. Benedict's followers were many, and to this day the Benedictines, both Catholic and Anglican, the oldest existing order of monks in the Western world, cherish Divine Reading as an integral part of everyday spiritual practice.

Divine Reading has survived over two thousand years because as a catalyst for dialogue with God, it works. You don't need to live outside city walls. All you need is your Bible and a quiet place.

Something the Benedictines take for granted, and that you for the moment should assume, is that you are not alone in the process

[3] From *The Rule of St. Benedict*, Prologue, Timothy Fry, ed. The Liturgical Press, Collegeville, MN, 1980.

of Divine Reading. God is wishing to speak to you. And so, you begin by inviting God to speak. Then imagine that the Scripture you are reading is a love letter from God written especially for you. The result of this simple shift in thinking will be an attitude of listening, rather than an atmosphere of study.

A substantive part of Divine Reading involves the use of periods of silence during which you listen for God's message to be revealed. Your patience with this process will bring its rewards. Divine Reading is a powerful tool, deceptive in its simplicity. As you struggle to find your way through your crisis, Divine Reading will pinpoint the issues you personally need to deal with and bring Scripture alive in a two-way form of communication.

This is the time to stop everything, to calm your feelings and relax your body. Read through the instructions that follow. Then ask God to speak to you through Divine Reading of a familiar passage—Psalm 23. As you read the words aloud, listen carefully to what God's Spirit may bring to your attention.

DIVINE READING

Listening to God Through Scripture

1. *Begin with prayer.* Your prayer can be as simple as "Lord, help me hear what you know I need to hear today."

2. *Read* your selected Scripture twice: the first time to familiarize yourself with the passage, the second time to listen.

   + During the second reading, listen for a word or a phrase that reaches out to you, that grabs you and shimmers in your mind's eye.
   + Hold on to the word or phrase in your memory. Do not analyze why you chose it. Merely observe it.

3. Now *be still and listen* to the thought that this word or phrase has generated. Spend at least two full minutes in quiet. If your thoughts wander, draw them back to the Scripture passage.

   + Jot down in a margin or on a "Reflections" page the part of Scripture that grabbed you.

4. *Read* the passage slowly again. The word or phrase that jumps out at you may or may not change. If a different portion catches your attention, make note of it. The spirit of God will lead you to the words you need. Ponder the words for a minimum of two minutes.

   + Observe what emotion the word or phrase creates in you. How does this part of Scripture connect with your life? Why does it hook you?

+ At the end of this time of quiet, write down just two things: the word or phrase that caught your attention this time and the emotion created in you.

5. *Read* the Scripture passage a final time, slowly and thoughtfully. You may return to the same word or phrase, you may be drawn in still a different direction. Remember, you are not alone in this process; you have invited God to work with you.

+ Sit silently for a longer period of time, at least four minutes.
+ As you reflect on your word or phrase and feel the emotions it generates, ask yourself, "If this is God's word to me now, what is God calling me to be or to do?" Stick with that question until you believe you have the answer.
+ At the end of your time of silence, write in your journal all that you have observed and experienced.

6. *Pray*. Conclude by thanking God for whatever you received. There will be rare instances when nothing insightful comes to your mind. Thank God for the quiet time.

Divine Reading in our church has become so meaningful that committee members often begin their meetings with it. Just as potent in a group setting, the process encourages individuals to internally examine issues in their lives, then learn further from the sharing.

Use Divine Reading to explore this Psalm.

THE 23RD PSALM

The LORD *is* my shepherd; I shall not want.
He maketh me to lie down in green
pastures: he leadeth me beside the still waters.
He restoreth my soul: he leadeth me in the paths of righteousness
for his name's sake.
Yea, though I walk through the valley of the shadow of death, I will
fear no evil:
for thou *art* with me; thy rod and thy staff they comfort me.

Thou preparest a table before me in the presence of mine enemies:
thou anointest my head with oil; my cup runneth over.
Surely goodness and mercy shall follow me all the days of my life:
and I will dwell in the house of the LORD for ever.

—KING JAMES VERSION

. . . .

. . . .

. . . .

. . . .

. . . .

. . . .

. . . .

. . . .

. . . .

. . . .

. . . .

. . . .

. . . .

. . . .

. . . .

. . . .

. . . .

. . . .

Now use Divine Reading to explore this translation.

THE 23RD PSALM

The LORD is my shepherd;
      I have everything I need.
He lets me rest in fields of green grass
      and leads me to quiet pools of
      fresh water.
He gives me new strength.
He guides me in the right paths,
      as he has promised.
Even if I go through the deepest
      darkness,
I will not be afraid, LORD,
      for you are with me.
Your shepherd's rod and staff
      protect me.

You prepare a banquet for me,
      where all my enemies can see
      me.
You welcome me as an honored
      guest
      and fill my cup to the brim.
I know that your goodness and love
      will be with me all my life;
      and your house will be my home
      as long as I live.

Based in Scripture, Divine Reading is simple, reasonable, and offers God an open heart and a mind ready to listen. Throughout this guide, you will find Scripture passages and prayers chosen specifically for this meditation technique. They will bolster you. Christians' doubts in times of trouble are as common as our individual troubles are unique—my pastor's robe certainly did not hold me immune from faltering faith, and in any case, communicating with God requires no religious title nor a doctorate in theology. Information, advice, solace, and companionship are there for the asking, from God, whose faith in us is never in crisis.

Now, before going on to Chapter 3, use Divine Reading to explore the role of God as your protector, the One who is beside you always.

*Take time to let Psalm 121 become a gift from God. Use Divine
Reading (page 29), and let your heart absorb the words and images.
Personalize the reading by substituting your own name for the name
"Israel." As a member of the body of Christ, you are a participant in the
"New Israel"—the church. So, this promise is for you.*

THE FAITHFULNESS OF GOD

I look to the mountains;
where will my help come from?
My help will come from the LORD,
who made heaven and earth.

He will not let you fall;
your protector is always awake.

The protector of Israel
never dozes or sleeps.
The LORD will guard you;
he is by your side to protect you.
The sun will not hurt you during the day,
nor the moon during the night.

The LORD will protect you from all danger;
he will keep you safe.
He will protect you as you come and go
now and forever.

—PSALMS 121

REFLECTIONS

3.

Ears of the Heart

◼

God whispers to us in our pleasures, speaks in our conscience, but shouts in our pains: it is his megaphone to rouse a deaf world.

—C. S. LEWIS, *PROBLEM OF PAIN*

My childhood, and probably yours, included learning to pray, and by the time I earned my doctorate I had every form of it down to an art—adoration, praise, thanksgiving, confession, petition, intercession, supplication. I could say grace, invocations, benedictions, and corporate prayers. I could guide group prayers. I could even sing a few.

What I had not learned to do was listen for a response.

Individual prayer, like Scripture, is a two-way pathway to God. Yet in all my studies I had missed that prayer meant a relationship with the One to whom I had always prayed. I had never once been taught to combine thoughts, dreams, yearnings, and desires with a sensitivity and awareness of God communicating back to me.

The summer just before my diagnosis I spent thirty days in silence at a Jesuit retreat house. It was admittedly an odd thing for me to do, on several counts. Being a natural extrovert, extended silence is contrary to my nature. I didn't work up to it gradually, I just went. I was also the only non-Catholic in residence.

What on earth made me do such a thing? On the rational side, after more than twenty-five years in ministry I was getting my first and quite possibly my only sabbatical. I wanted that time to make a difference in my life. And emotionally, I needed to recapture the idealism and zeal that had propelled me into ministry in the first place. I had never wanted to be a church bureaucrat or a fund-raiser or a designer of programs and buildings. I had said yes to ministry because I had fallen in love with God, but over the years the practical demands of the job had tarnished the luster of that love relationship. I simply didn't want to go to one more conference and learn more techniques on how to manage a church. I wanted to rediscover the *something* that was missing.

So I headed to the Jesuit retreat center in Los Altos, California—a place of rolling hills, olive groves, oak trees, rudimentary living, and utterly no distractions. There were other participants on the retreat, but you wouldn't have known it: We were instructed not to look each other in the eye. One evening in the dining hall I stood up to get a cup of coffee and realized I couldn't find my table again—I had no idea who was sitting with me. Common courtesy fell by the wayside; not even a "Please pass the salt" fell from anyone's lips. It was isolation as I'd never known it, and I buried myself in intense self-examination and scriptural study. There, in that silence, I learned the spiritual exercises of the Jesuits' founder, Ignatius Loyola.

Ignatius Loyola was born in the Basque region of Northern Spain in 1491. Tradition at the time held that a youth of good family was sent to a noble and preferably royal household for a thorough education, so at fifteen, Ignatius arrived at the fortress home of Juan Velásquez de Cuéllar, Treasurer of Castile. There his lessons included the subject of warfare. He aspired to be a knight and spent his early life as a soldier.

Ignatius was prone to reckless gambling, affairs with women, dueling, drinking, and brawling. It wasn't until he was wounded at age thirty and came face-to-face with his own death that his relationship with God came alive. During a battle with the French, not far from Pamplona, a cannonball flew between his legs, shattering the right leg and leaving gaping wounds in the left. Medics from the French military, out of admiration for the way Ignatius had led the Spanish troops, set the bones in his right leg and dressed his wounds. Given the limitations of surgery on the battlefield in the sixteenth century, Ignatius was fortunate to have avoided amputation.

Nearly two weeks after his injury, Ignatius was taken by litter to the home of his sister, Magdalena, where his condition worsened. More than a month after the initial injury, physicians and surgeons agreed that either the French had bungled the job or that the bones had shifted on the long journey to Magdalena's home. The leg was broken again and the bones reset. The strain of the operation and the considerable accompanying pain brought Ignatius so close to death that he was advised to make his last confession. A priest was summoned. Four days later Ignatius was told that if he were no better by that midnight he could count himself a dead man. Ignatius prayed, promising to devote his skills as a knight to the service of God should he recover, and a change is reported to have occurred at 12 midnight. By 3 A.M., he was out of danger.

Although Ignatius survived, this second operation also proved to have gone badly wrong. When the bones grew together, a stump protruded from his right leg. Through a series of events, Ignatius agreed to yet a third operation. He was informed that it would be more painful than anything he had previously endured, as the protruding bone would have to be taken off with a saw. Despite the impending torture, Ignatius chose to proceed with the third surgery, after which he spent four days in a traction device that was little more than the medieval rack.

It took Ignatius nearly a year to recover. During that long convalescence, he immersed himself in two books, both popular classics of the time. The first was *The Life of Christ*, written by the Carthusian monk Ludolph of Saxony, translated into Spanish and printed in four volumes starting in 1502. The second, *Lives of the Saints*, was by the Italian Dominican Jacopo de Voragine, Archbishop of Genoa, who died in 1298. Through these works, God changed both Ignatius' life and the world. By the time Ignatius had mended enough to leave his place of recovery and begin to pick up the pieces of his life, he had heard God's call. He committed himself to become a knight for Christ, took his vows, and dedicated the rest of his days to serving the poor.[1]

Ignatius' new devotion to God and his background as a highly trained soldier proved a fascinating combination. He believed that, just as physical exercise created better soldiers, spiritual exercise would help people become better Christians. He soon developed (or received from God) a series of exercises designed specifically to bring a person closer in relationship with the Creator. The complete exercises, which required a full month of prolonged prayer, were eventually compiled into a small book. It was this book that attracted his first religious companions and to this day serves as a benchmark in our Christian religion.

Ignatius' life remained colorful: He traveled extensively, advanced his formal education, was arrested, tried, and eventually released by authorities of the Spanish Inquisition, and by all accounts never wavered from his commitment to the destitute. He formally founded the Society of Jesus in Rome in 1540, and established missions in such far-flung regions as Brazil, the Congo, India, and Japan.

[1] *Ignatius Loyola: A Biography of the Founder of the Jesuits*, by Philip Caraman. Harper & Row Publishers, New York, 1990.

Excessive penance for the sins of his youth permanently damaged his health, and he died in 1556. The Catholic church canonized him in 1622.

His book, *Spiritual Exercises*, is rough and profoundly simple and can still be found in print, its final revisions having been made in 1541. It is not a book to be read, but a meditation guide, a method to be practiced. A key to the method is imagination, since during his lengthy recovery Ignatius had been forced to entertain himself. Being a romantic, he had imagined tales of great valor with noble knights doing battle, or passionate stories about beautiful ladies. Likewise he let his imagination run as he read about Christ's life and the great saints of the early years of Christianity. In the process, he realized that the more fanciful tales quickly faded from memory, while his imaginings of Christ and the saints grew richer and communicated deep truths.

Ignatius discovered what was to become central to his spiritual practice: God can work powerfully through our imagination if we invite God to do so. Imagination is so important that I prefer to call these spiritual practices *Imaginative Prayer*. The term "exercise" is misleading today in any case, bringing to mind an awful lot of work when Ignatius himself counseled tranquil prayer and peaceful meditations that required no effort at all.

There is a pattern to Imaginative Prayer; the basic process is easy to learn and I have found it can be adapted in multiple ways (Ignatius was never one for hard and fast rules). The results of these meditations vary from a calm and comforting sense of the presence of God to experiences that can be quite startling. Though it didn't happen right away, it was through this process that God flagged down my attention, setting off a chain of events and revealing my illness. It has been this process that has given me hope for true healing.

Starting on the following pages, I invite you to experience Imaginative Prayer for yourself, using the well-known story of Jesus healing a paralytic, found in Luke 5:17–26. Thoughts, visions, sounds, dreams—as you listen for God, be open for responses that are uniquely yours. As I remember my own encounters with God and write them here in the chapters that follow, it is clear they have never taken the same form twice. Effective reading of Scripture and effective prayer are not matters of achieving some correct attitude and receiving a prescribed response. As Augustine said, prayer is less the soul's striving and more a "holy longing, submitting to be remade by God." Our hope, then, is not in a singular, proper technique as we seek God. Our hope is in the God who is already seeking us.

Hearing God's Response

Preparation:

+ Choose a comfortable position.
+ Have with you your Bible, your writing material, and a watch.
+ Set aside approximately 15–30 minutes.

1. *Begin with a prayer* of preparation, offering this experience to God: "Lord, grant me your grace that all my thoughts, all my feelings, all my actions, all my interactions might be ordered to glorify and serve your divine will."

2. *Read with imagination* the chosen passage of Scripture several times. Picture the setting, the people, buildings. Imagine the looks on people's faces and the emotions they had. Picture Jesus. Be as specific as possible.

3. *State what you desire* from God. The more specific you can be with your desire, the better. A possible desire for this passage might be: "Lord, I desire a deeper knowledge of you and your healing power."

[Steps 1–3 normally take a total of 3 to 5 minutes.]

4. *Meditate.* Imagine yourself as being one of the characters, then watch the story unfold in your mind. Imagine the sights, sounds, and smells, the dialogue, people's reactions. Let the story take on a

life of its own. If you become distracted or your mind begins to wander, go back and pick up the story. Be aware of the feelings you experience. Remember that you have offered this time to God, that you have invited God to work with you.

[This step will normally take 80–85 percent of your allotted time.]

5. *Summarize in prayer* your experience and thank God for whatever you have received. It may be helpful to imagine this section as the summation of a telephone call with a friend—Jesus. You could tell him what you appreciate and raise any questions that are lingering from your time together. You might let him know when you would like to talk with him again.

   Enjoy this time and continue to listen carefully. I found this a part of the process in which God was particularly active. If you experienced nothing but a time of quiet, thank God for that. As always, we do not control how and when God works.

6. Conclude with the Lord's Prayer.

7. You may find it helpful to write down any thoughts or insights you had during the meditation. I find that God often works as much in the writing as in the meditation.

Use Imaginative Prayer (page 44).

JESUS HEALS A PARALYZED MAN

One day when Jesus was teaching, some Pharisees and teachers of the Law were sitting there who had come from every town in Galilee and Judea and from Jerusalem. The power of the LORD was present for Jesus to heal the sick. Some men came carrying a paralyzed man on a bed, and they tried to carry him into the house and put him in front of Jesus. Because of the crowd, however, they could find no way to take him in. So they carried him up on the roof, made an opening in the tiles, and let him down on his bed into the middle of the group in front of Jesus. When Jesus saw how much faith they had, he said to the man, "Your sins are forgiven, my friend."

The teachers of the Law and the Pharisees began to say to themselves, "Who is this man who speaks such blasphemy! God is the only one who can forgive sins!"

Jesus knew their thoughts and said to them, "Why do you think such things? Is it easier to say, 'Your sins are forgiven you,' or to say, 'Get up and walk'? I will prove to you, then, that the Son of Man has authority on earth to forgive sins." So he said to the paralyzed man, "I tell you, get up, pick up your bed, and go home!"

At once the man got up in front of them all, took the bed he had been lying on, and went home, praising God. They were all completely amazed! Full of fear, they praised God, saying, "What marvelous things we have seen today!"

—LUKE 5:17–26

Before going on to Chapter 4, use Imaginative Prayer (page 44) to recognize your exhaustion and your need for renewed strength. Picture specifically what renewed strength would enable you to do, if God were to give it to you. Imagine what it would take to make you feel joyfully energetic. Let the words of Isaiah become a personal message from God to you.

MEDITATION ON RENEWED STRENGTH

Don't you know? Haven't you heard?
The LORD is the everlasting God;
    he created all the world.
He never grows tired or weary.
No one understands his thoughts.
He strengthens those who are weak and tired.
Even those who are young grow weak;
    young people can fall exhausted.
But those who trust in the LORD for help
    will find their strength renewed.
They will rise on wings like eagles;
    they will run and not get weary;
    they will walk and not grow weak.

—ISAIAH 40:28–31

4.

LISTENING TO GOD

■

May you be blessed forever, Lord, for putting up with such a stubborn soul as mine.

—TERESA OF AVILA, SPAIN (1515–82)

I inherited my Midwestern ancestors' skepticism toward anything that smacks of the mystical. The dreams, the voices, the strange events that people might confide to me in the past only prompted me to pull out my Iowa practicality and wave it like a banner—especially when some well-intended person began, "God told me to tell you . . ."

But by that summer of my twenty-fifth year on the job, I was wanting God dreadfully. Though the Jesuit retreat sounds like some form of self-inflicted punishment, I thought by shutting off one form of communication, which seemed of late to get in the way of my own spirituality, I could open the door to communion with God. So I was drawn to thirty days in silence, a journey into the wilderness of my own soul to wait and see if God would act. Though my goals were vague, my desire was clear and strong: I wanted to reignite my relationship with the Divine.

And it did reignite, although not right away and certainly not in any form I could have expected, given my skeptical nature.

The retreat started out logically. The Jesuits assigned each of us a spiritual director, the only person with whom we could speak, and handed out daily spiritual exercises in the form of Imaginative Prayer. The first week's exercises were on sin, a tough focus for me, since I was still euphoric about actually getting a month off work. But the high quickly faded, as one might imagine, given such heavy material. Day three, steeped in the meditations on sin, I was slightly depressed and feeling a strong urge to find a pay phone and talk to loved ones. A predictable response to missing home, I thought.

By day six, the prescribed exercises had wound their way to intense, imaginative perceptions of hell—the sound (the wails), the smell (carrion), the taste (like vomit), the feel (the blisters) of hell. I was wallowing in black depression. If I had wanted to feel this badly about my life's course and everybody else's, I needn't have traveled to a retreat center to do it. Why was I here?

The next day I found out. That seventh day I was broadsided by a surging anger: at the church that proclaims the gospel that God's love is offered unconditionally to all, then goes about making rules about who is really acceptable; at my job, so tangled in an unending web of bureaucracy that I had no time to be of real use to my Lord. I hadn't known how seriously I had been thinking of leaving my profession, and there, revealed to the light, was my true fear and the real reason that I had come: that I was ready to give up, quit the church altogether—the church through which I had come to know Jesus, the only way I knew to serve Christ.

Suddenly, I heard from nowhere, "Charles, are you trying to divorce me?"

The startling voice of my Lord in my ear was the first of many odd occurrences that shook my being throughout the remainder of my thirty days: Clear, mental pictures of Jesus' boyhood. Griping despair in meditations on Gethsemane. Wonder at a body gone missing. And more words from God: how I was to serve, where I was to serve, expectations that focused at times on areas of ministry I didn't much like.

I don't know what impression I left on my spiritual director. He expressed nothing but compassion as my skepticism about the effects of Ignatian meditation dissolved into a series of stammering reports. I wouldn't blame him, though, if he felt a bit satisfied and perhaps even amused at how my Iowa farm boy Protestant practicality had transformed itself.

I did emerge changed from the experience. I knew clearly where God wanted me and though I wasn't altogether happy yet about the decision, I had found my way through what I deemed was the "wilderness of my soul," and I was open to hear God speaking to me.

In hindsight, I didn't know what wilderness really was. In my illness, I know now. In hindsight, my previous wholesale skepticism of other people's encounters with God—particularly during crisis—looks a bit foolish.

Today, I have only to remember the story of a trusted professor and friend, Dr. Howard Rice, to be humbled all over again. Howard was already a noted author and theologian when I first met him thirty years ago. He was also already in a wheelchair, living with a diagnosis of multiple sclerosis. The diagnosis first came down when he was still in his early thirties, married, with two children, and having trouble walking. Minus the benefit of today's MRI technology, physicians launched into a series of miserably painful spinal taps—and with each one, Howard's condition went downhill. They injected dyes into his brain, looking for tumors. Finally, neurologists termed it MS and without any viable treatment options, showed him the door.

"It was a slow process, the loss of control of my lower body,"

Howard says. "First I used canes, then crutches, and finally I fell down a flight of stairs and that was it. I was never able to stand up again. The memory is blurry—I guess I've blocked it. I remember asking the doctor, 'Why couldn't it be a brain tumor?' He said, 'I wish it were.' One neurologist simply said, 'Don't bother me. I can't do anything for you. Don't come back.'

"I wanted to die. I deliberately smoked two packs of cigarettes a day. I thought I'd rather die of lung cancer than become a vegetable where you can't move or dress or feed yourself, or even speak."

The low point came not long after Howard was confined to the chair: "All my rage came out. I yelled and cursed and called God every name in the book. I tore the wheels off the chair—I tore it as much as I could, to pieces, until I was exhausted, lying on the floor, sobbing.

"And then I heard God say to me, 'It's okay, Howard. I love you.'"

No cataclysmic event. No ability to stand up and walk. But at that point, Howard says he was filled with a miraculous sense of hope.

I heard Howard first tell this story years ago, before my illness. Was it because Howard was still in a wheelchair that I at the time mentally filed his account of God's response as metaphor? Or was it a more basic reason—that I hadn't yet sought the literal God?

I have come to believe that the desire to go on that retreat was nothing less than my own gift from God. The color, the clarity of my summer meditations refused to fade after I was back on the job. I reread my journals and carved out time for my prayers, and it was just months later, while practicing Imaginative Prayer, that I had the meditation experience that would save my life.

It was autumn, and I had made it clear to my family that there was no chance any of us were going up to my parents' home in Oregon for Thanksgiving—it was just too costly. Then, on the night of October 28, my father called: His prostate cancer, supposedly eradicated by radiation eight years before, had reappeared. The next morning, distracted and upset, I took my worries to my Lord.

I used a variation of Imaginative Prayer, and though most often this exercise leaves me with nothing more than a quiet sense of the presence of God, this meditation unfolded in a way that caught me unprepared.

First, I offered the time to God and expressed my desire: to understand and accept God's future for my father. Then, in my imagination, I went to my own private beach (a place I had created in my mind) to speak with Jesus. As usual, he came. It was, after all, my meditation and I was creating the mental images—or so I thought. This morning, however, Jesus seemed distant. To my surprise, he was preoccupied. Here, from my journal, are the events that followed:

Though Jesus seemed to have something else on his mind, I talked to him about my concerns for my father. He just listened. Suddenly and unexpectedly, from behind me my father appeared. He walked past me and went right over to Jesus. They greeted one another, embraced, turned, and starting walking away from me down the beach! In disbelief, I watched them as they walked away together, my dad stooped and shuffling his feet as he does. It was obvious they were glad to be together. My father stopped, turned back, and looked at me, happy and contented. He smiled and waved, then turned back around and walked away with Jesus! I was left alone on the beach. I cannot remember a more lonely feeling in my life.

I wept. Later, when I had collected myself enough to begin my prayer of summation, I asked God, "What does this all mean?" In my mind, I heard clearly the answer, "He is mine." From within me, my own silent voice yelled, "But what about me? He is mine, too!" Then I heard God again, "He is mine, just as you are mine. You have always known this would not be forever. Trust me." I wrote:

I understand in my head; I feel an incredible loneliness in my heart. I don't depend on my father for much that is tangible. I do assume that he is "head" of our family, and I don't know how I feel about myself being the oldest generation. I do love and trust God. I do suspect that the day will come when my dad and I will be together and not worrying about things like cancer and death. I do know that he and I will be okay. Jesus needed to focus on my dad more than on me. For that I am glad—lonely but glad.

I was on the phone to the airlines immediately. Come Thanksgiving, on the plane I opened my mind to God through meditation again. There, in the middle of that flight, inside my head, I heard a clear message: "You are where I want you."

While the meditation experiences I had were unusual, I do not believe they are rare. I believe the God who created us, the God who loves us more than we love ourselves, desires to come *to each one of us*. Our challenge is not to cause the arrival, but only to open our hearts and minds to listen to God. It is important to remember, though, that no matter how hard we practice, meditation does not manipulate God into coming. God is not a cosmic bellhop who shows up when we ring.

When God comes, there are no words to adequately describe the impact. For me, though that October morning's meditation eventually led to a frightening revelation, I look back on it now with incredible wonder and thanksgiving. If I had not had the experience of that meditation, if I had not listened to the message, if I had not responded and arranged to make the Thanksgiving trip to Oregon, then I would not have heard a doctor's challenge to me that would prolong my life.

For during that unplanned visit, my mother, my sister, and I went with my father to work out his treatment program. The doctor gave us a brilliant and very caring one-hour lecture. He left out nothing: the nature of prostate cancer, prostate specific antigen (PSA) tests (for possible presence of prostate cancer), Gleason scores (that measure the cancer's virulence), and possible treatments. Given our family's health history, the diagnosis was not all that surprising and due to my father's advanced age, the cancer's progression could well be slow enough that his eventual death would most likely be due to something else altogether.

When he finished, the doctor turned to me and said, "Now you get yourself checked out. You're in a high-risk category."

I thought, "I exercise, I watch what I eat, I meditate . . . I have no symptoms—why do I need a test?" But to the doctor I said, "Good idea." I went in to my doctor two days later, on December 1. The diagnosis was confirmed in January. Surgery was in February. The rest is history. It was all a total, awful surprise.

*Remember your journey before you leave this chapter. Use Divine
Reading (page 29), Imaginative Prayer (page 44), or both.*

A CRY FOR HELP

LORD God, my savior, I cry out all day,
and at night I come before you.
Hear my prayer;
listen to my cry for help!

So many troubles have fallen on me
that I am close to death.
I am like all others who are about to die;
all my strength is gone.

I am abandoned among the dead;
I am like the slain lying in their graves,
those you have forgotten
completely,
who are beyond your help.
You have thrown me into the
depths of the tomb,
into the darkest and deepest pit.
Your anger lies heavy on me,
and I am crushed beneath its
waves. . . .

LORD, I call to you for help;
every morning I pray to you.
Why do you reject me, LORD?
Why do you turn away from me?

—PSALMS 88:1–7, 13–14

Now let Psalm 91 become God's gift to you. Using Divine Reading (page 29), Imaginative Prayer (page 44), or both, let the words and images of this Psalm soak in. Since it is obvious that all bodies eventually experience death, when you come to the references about death and disaster hear these words in the context of Jesus' promise of a life that transcends the death of the body.
Savor these promises.

GOD OUR PROTECTOR

Whoever goes to the LORD for safety,
whoever remains under the
protection of the Almighty,
can say to him,
"You are my defender and
protector.
You are my God; in you I trust."
He will keep you safe from all
hidden dangers
and from all deadly diseases.
He will cover you with his wings;
you will be safe in his care;
his faithfulness will protect and
defend you.
You need not fear any dangers at
night
or sudden attacks during the day
or the plagues that strike in the
dark
or the evils that kill in daylight.

A thousand may fall dead beside
you,
ten thousand all around you,
but you will not be harmed.
You will look and see
how the wicked are punished.

You have made the Lord your
defender,
the Most High your protector,
and so no disaster will strike you,
no violence will come near your
home.
God will put his angels in charge
of you
to protect you wherever you go.
They will hold you up with their
hands
to keep you from hurting your
feet on the stones.
You will trample down lions and
snakes,
fierce lions and poisonous
snakes.

God says, "I will save those who
love me
and will protect those who
acknowledge me as Lord.
When they call to me, I will answer
them;
when they are in trouble, I will
be with them.

I will rescue them and honor them.
I will reward them with long life;
I will save them."

—PSALMS 91

REFLECTIONS

Spend time listening to Jesus' promise that you will never be alone. Use Divine Reading (page 29) to explore the passage from John on this page. Spend a minimum of fifteen minutes in silence with this passage and let it become your own.

THE PROMISE OF DIVINE PRESENCE

"Do not be worried and upset," Jesus told them. . . . "The Helper, the Holy Spirit, whom the Father will send in my name, will teach you everything and make you remember all that I have told you. Peace is what I leave with you; it is my own peace that I give you. I do not give it as the world does. Do not be worried and upset; do not be afraid."

—JOHN 14:1, 26–27

REFLECTIONS

A prayer to simply read. Let the words become your own.

A Prayer of Giving Thanks

Lord, you come to us in such mysterious ways. You come to us through the words of Scripture. You come to us through the Living Word, your Son, Jesus Christ. You come to us through the words of others. You come to us through the words and thoughts of our own minds. You come to us through the yearnings and feelings of our hearts.

I do not understand how you come. I do not know why you come to me. I just know that you do come.

Thank you for still coming, O Lord. Help me always desire you. Give me ears to hear you. Give me motivation to respond to you. For I am yours, O Lord. I am yours.

—CHARLES SHIELDS

REFLECTIONS

5.

AVALANCHE OF EMOTIONS

■

The diagnosis was like a Fellini movie, dark and bizarre. My husband Charles had gone in for tests and the results were due back the next day. When we went out to dinner with friends that night, I was marveling that Charles was business as usual, with this news hanging over our heads. We got home late and I was washing my face when I said, "Well, I guess we'll hear back from the doctor tomorrow."

Charles said, "No, he called this afternoon." I stood there. He said, "It's malignant." I leaned against the wall, then I sank to the floor—I couldn't seem to carry my weight. I said, "Why didn't you tell me earlier?" He said, "You wouldn't have made it through dinner." We went to bed a little later. Neither of us slept very much. I was awake most of the night, crying most of the night.

—NADIA SHIELDS

My crisis could have been some other physical failure: heart attack, stroke, a debilitating disease, or an accident. The nature of the crisis, in the end, doesn't really matter. There is a song by Shawn Colvin called "Shotgun Down the Avalanche" and I cannot imagine a better phrase to describe the aftermath of anyone's devastating diagnosis—life out of control; test after test coming down with more bad news. The weight of decisions to be made bears down right on top of us and, though we may not be in a position to recognize it, on top of people we love. For a little while I hid it well, but the news had exploded inside of me, touching off my own avalanche of emotion.

My first response was immobilizing shock. I could not believe the diagnosis could possibly be true. But multiple confirmations quickly transformed the denial into anger, and then I was incredibly angry, with nowhere to focus the fury. I could not get mad at the members of my family; it was not their fault I had cancer. I could not get mad at the people I worked with—it was not their fault, either. So at times I focused on myself: What did I do to bring this on? What should I have done to recognize, to waylay this disease? And I focused on God: Why would God lead me to a doctor only to deliver what felt like a death sentence? I had been betrayed by my own body, betrayed by a personal physician who should have looked for the tumor earlier . . . betrayed by God?

So shock became disbelief, disbelief became denial, denial became anger, and through it all ran fear. The passions raged, shaking my faith and throwing into doubt all I had ever believed.

Where is the God who comes? Where is God at the time of our greatest need? On top of that, that summer I had just spent thirty days in silent meditation and prayer, all the time receiving no clue from God that a tumor was inside me, growing. My anger at God only added guilt to all my other emotions—and I felt utterly isolated. Then I remembered the psalmist, who more than once, in human anguish, dares to blame God.

Now, as I read the psalmist, Job, Jesus in the garden, Paul with his "thorn in the flesh," I know I am hardly the first to have such feelings. Imagine the loneliness and desperation of the woman who, after twelve years of an illness that made her "unclean," would dare to touch the hem of Jesus' robe. Imagine the anger and loneliness of Mob, who wandered the tombs, screaming in his illness until Jesus drove the "evil spirits" away. Imagine the depression and hopelessness of the man by the pool of Bethesda who for thirty-eight years had no one willing to put him in the water. Talk about feeling betrayed and alone.

If reminders from Scripture were not comfort enough, shortly after my diagnosis I received a letter from Bruce Gossard, a member of our congregation. Bruce had grown up with a generic Christian faith and as with many young people he searched and experimented during his teenage years. God was present but not foremost in Bruce's mind. That is, until Bruce was nineteen years old and a rattlesnake bite sent him to the hospital. His letter recorded his memories:

> I got to the hospital within fifteen minutes. But during the night, my leg swelled, cutting off circulation to my foot. Gangrene set in. During the next six months, as I lay in the hospital alternately in pain or stupefied by narcotics, I gradually lost several toes and, finally, my lower leg about eight inches below the knee. During the long nights alone, I mourned bitterly:

> SUMMER'S END
> (THOUGHTS AT AGE 19)

> So now I'll live a one-legged life.
> With no love and no one to be my wife.
> What good am I, just half a man?
> A cripple, a beggar with outstretched hand?

Baseball and football are gone for me;
And even golf is history.
Skiing at Mammoth is over, too.
What the hell did I ever do?

I think I'd rather just be dead
Than to face this future full of dread.
Did I deserve this wretched fate?
If there is a god, he's a god of hate!

—BRUCE GOSSARD

Bruce's feelings hit him with the intensity of that same avalanche, and in his loneliness there was no one to vent his emotions to but God. So, like a modern-day psalmist, Bruce raged at God.

When Jesus faced the final crisis of his life he did the same. In the agony of the garden we are told that, with sweat falling from his brow like great drops of blood, Jesus prayed, "Let this cup pass from me." In other words, *I don't want this to be happening!* I can imagine Jesus yelling, as I so often did, "No! No! No!"

Later, on the cross, our Lord was overheard praying the Psalms, the prayer book of the people of God. He prayed, "My God, my God, why have you abandoned me?" Had we heard him go on, he would have continued, "I have cried desperately for help, but still it does not come." If Jesus meant what he was saying, even he was blaming God in that moment of human helplessness.

Take this moment to explore Psalm 22 on the following page. Use Imaginative Prayer to identify with Jesus' crisis and the emotions that he might have experienced as he hung on the cross.

Use Imaginative Prayer (page 44) to identify with the emotions Jesus may have experienced during his crisis.

MEDITATION ON ABANDONMENT

My God, my God, why have
you abandoned me?
I have cried desperately for help,
but still it does not come.
During the day I call to you, my
God,
but you do not answer;
I call at night,
but get no rest.
But you are enthroned as the
Holy One,
the One whom Israel praises.
Our ancestors put their trust in
you;
they trusted you, and you saved
them.
They called to you and escaped
from danger;
they trusted you and were not
disappointed.
But I am no longer a human being;
I am a worm,
despised and scorned by
everyone!
All who see me make fun of me;

they stick out their tongues and
shake their heads.
"You relied on the LORD," they say.
"Why doesn't he save you?
If the LORD likes you,
why doesn't he help you?"

It was you who brought me safely
through birth,
and when I was a baby, you
kept me safe.
I have relied on you since the day I
was born,
and you have always been my
God.
Do not stay away from me!
Trouble is near,
and there is no one to help.

—PSALMS 22:1–11

As people of faith we have a place to take our intense feelings, even if they are feelings of anger or hatred. Letting God know what we are feeling is one of the healthiest things we can do, and in the midst of that confession, we will find we have a God who hears our words and doesn't run away. We will find a God who hears and heals anyway. God can deal with our feelings of betrayal in a way no human can ever do. God can handle our disbelief, our denial, our inner conflicts (God's people have always been filled with conflict; the very name "Israel" means literally "One who wrestles with God"). No personal story illustrates this more powerfully than that of John and Sue Kunz.

The Reverend Dr. John Kunz heads a community church for a little town in a fold of the Sierra Nevada mountains. One December, his thirty-six-year-old wife, Sue, asked to stop by the chiropractic office of a family friend. The visit was routine, the result was not: Her neck manipulation went wrong, triggering what was later diagnosed as a brain stem stroke. John, horrified, saw his wife's brain shut down before his eyes.

"The chiropractor adjusted her neck, then left the room," says John. "Sue said, 'I'm so dizzy . . .'" Her voice faded. John said, "Who are you?" She said, "I am Sue."

"Where do you live?"

"Big Creek."

"How many children do you have?"

(whisper) "Four."

"Then she was gone," John says. "We went from a totally normal, gung-ho family to totally stopped. I was sitting right there. I watched it happen." The ambulance came screaming down the street, while in the parking lot Sue and John's two youngest children waited to go Christmas shopping.

Sue went into a deep coma. News spread instantly through the shocked community and the hospital was swamped for days with people who came and stayed, and prayed. Sue was given eight hours to live, but she did not die. Neither did she come out of the coma, and at last a hospital neurologist called to request Sue be moved out of the acute care facility. John, bewildered, asked where he should take her: "The doctor told me, 'I suggest you take her out in the parking lot, let her catch pneumonia and die.' He crushed me like a bulldozer."

John rallied to battle on. Sue Kunz at last regained consciousness, and though seven years of intensive therapy created only minimal mobility and barely intelligible speech, mentally she is today 95 percent of what she had been prior to the stroke.

"Sue's faith is fine and strong," says John. It is his own faith he questions. "One day while we were still at the hospital I was reading John 11, the part where Lazarus had died and Jesus resurrected him. I prayed, 'Lord, resurrect her, or take her,' and I was so confident God was going to do one of those right then, I actually reached for the phone. I expected the medical staff to call me and say, 'Something has happened . . .' I reached for the phone, but the phone did not ring."

Habits die hard, and John continued through weeks and months with a stream of what he assumed were unanswered prayers. One day, however, he connected: " 'God, where are you? I know we live in an out-of-the-way place, but why have you forgotten me?' Then I thought I heard God answer, 'I am out at your place right now, in the woman who came to help from nine in the morning to eleven, the one who will be there from eleven to one, from one to three, and three to five.' "

God's hands and feet were already in the Kunz household, in the people who came to help. God's voice was already present, in the phone calls from loved ones who would say, "How are you, honestly?" In reply to God, John prayed again, "You haven't forgotten me. You haven't spoken audibly in my ear, you haven't sent an angel in glorious form—any of those things we want—but you have come in your people. Here you are."

Though John's faith in God had faltered, God was at work. And yet, who cannot relate to John's need for reassurance? However we express ourselves, in quiet prayers, shouts to God or silent misery, we are not alone in the emotions we are facing . . . virtually every person whose life has been shaken by physical crisis has felt the same way. Jesus and the psalmist did. So did Paul. On the following page, read Paul's magnificent description in Romans of the conflict and pain in creation itself—pain so fierce that all creation can do is groan like a woman in childbirth. Recognize the feelings you have, especially if they are of hurt so intense that words cannot express them. Perhaps all you can do is groan and then trust God.

There are times when we don't have words to express the emotions we are experiencing—the feelings are too intense. Use Divine Reading (page 29) to let these words reach into your heart.

FEELINGS BEYOND WORDS

I consider that what we suffer at this present time cannot be compared at all with the glory that is going to be revealed to us.... For we know that up to the present time all of creation groans with pain, like the pain of childbirth.... the Spirit comes to help us, weak as we are. For we do not know how we ought to pray; the Spirit himself pleads with God for us in groans that words cannot express. And God, who sees into our hearts, knows what the thought of the Spirit is.

—ROMANS 8:18, 22, 26–27

REFLECTIONS

Whatever feelings you have, God will not run away. If you are angry, God can take your anger. If you are confused and full of conflict, who better to invite into your own personal chaos than the One who can calm storms? Even if you feel betrayed and temporarily reject God, share your emotions with God. Like the father of the prodigal son, God knows that the rejection is not permanent. God, like the father in Jesus' parable, has demonstrated over and over the willingness to patiently wait for you to work through your feelings, and the loving longing for you to return home. During the moments I questioned a God who could let this happen to me, it was not God who had changed; the avalanche of feelings had clouded my awareness and my trust, and it was I who had changed, inside.

The suddenly unleashed emotions swooped down with a life of their own and carried me along in a torrent that threatened to wipe me out. And of all the emotions, one loomed larger than all the rest, the hardest to put aside, the darkest to walk through. It was, of course, fear. In my own journey, for all my meditations and prayers, fear still got the better of me. Beyond the anger, the desperation and betrayal, I was afraid of what might come. I was frightened that I might not be able to see my daughters through school. I was frightened that I had not adequately provided for my family.

I was afraid to die.

The emotions that accompany crisis generally do not all come at one time, but rather in waves. You may wish to return periodically to the following Scripture passage as you work through your own avalanche of feelings. For this Psalm, define your internal enemies, then use Divine Reading (page 29), Imaginative Prayer (page 44), or both.

A PRAYER OF FRUSTRATION

How much longer will you
forget me, LORD?
Forever?
How much longer will you hide
yourself from me?
How long must I endure trouble?
How long will sorrow fill my
heart day and night?
How long will my enemies
triumph over me?

Look at me, O LORD my God,
and answer me.
Restore my strength; don't let
me die.

—PSALMS 13:1–3

REFLECTIONS

. . . .

. . . .

. . . .

. . . .

. . . .

. . . .

. . . .

. . . .

. . . .

. . . .

. . . .

. . . .

. . . .

. . . .

. . . .

. . . .

. . . .

Use Divine Reading (page 29), Imaginative Prayer (page 44), or both to bring this prayer alive.

A PRAYER FOR HELP

Listen to me, LORD, and answer me,
for I am helpless and weak.
Save me from death, because I am
loyal to you;
save me, for I am your servant
and I trust in you.

You are my God, so be merciful
to me;
I pray to you all day long.
Make your servant glad, O LORD,
because my prayers go up
to you.
You are good to us and forgiving,
full of constant love for all who
pray to you.

Listen, LORD, to my prayer;
hear my cries for help.
I call to you in times of trouble,
because you answer my prayers.

—PSALMS 86:1—7

Whenever anger, frustration, despair, or fear becomes overwhelming, read the following promises from Scripture. Select a passage and read it over three times, allowing at least two minutes of silence in between each reading. Let it become a personal promise from God to you. Begin each meditation time inviting God to speak to you and conclude by giving thanks for whatever you received.

PROMISES FROM SCRIPTURE

"I have called you by name—you are mine."
—ISAIAH 43:1

"Do not be afraid—I am with you!"
—ISAIAH 41:10

"I will never leave you; I will never abandon you."
—HEBREWS 13:5

"I will be with you always, to the end of the age."
—MATTHEW 28:20

"I am the bread of life."
—JOHN 6:48

"I am the light of the world."
—JOHN 8:12

"I am the good shepherd . . . I know my sheep. . . ."
—JOHN 10:14–15

"Come to me, all of you who are tired from carrying heavy loads, and I will give you rest."
—MATTHEW 11:28

"God's free gift is eternal life in union with Christ Jesus our Lord."

—ROMANS 6:23

"Nothing . . . will ever be able to separate us from the love of God which is ours through Christ Jesus our Lord."

—ROMANS 8:39

Before going on to Chapter 6, simply read and remember.

ANCIENT WORDS OF HOPE

Here on Mount Zion the LORD Almighty will prepare a banquet for all the nations of the world—a banquet of the richest food and the finest wine. Here he will suddenly remove the cloud of sorrow that has been hanging over all the nations. The Sovereign LORD will destroy death forever! He will wipe away the tears from everyone's eyes and take away the disgrace his people have suffered throughout the world. The LORD himself has spoken.

When it happens, everyone will say, "He is our God! We have put our trust in him, and he has rescued us. He is the LORD! We have put our trust in him, and now we are happy and joyful because he has saved us."

—ISAIAH 25:6–9

6.

THE VIEW FROM
THE VALLEY OF SHADOWS

---

*Yea, though I walk through the valley of the shadow of death, I will
fear no evil...*

—PSALMS 23:4, KING JAMES VERSION

Walk? I wasn't walking through the valley of the shadows. I was
slipping, tripping, sliding, crawling, stumbling—everything but
walking. Of all the emotions, all the fears I was encountering, by far
the strongest was the fear of death. Death was too close, too permanent, and I didn't want to be facing it.

My fear of death was ironic. Ministering to the dying, after all,
is something I have done and still do all the time. Nevertheless, in
the face of my own deadly disease a cure was what I desperately
wanted. And I knew all too well there are times when no cure comes.
Bernadette Catlin is just one example.

Bernadette was both a parishioner and a friend. By the time she and I met, she had already given up her nursing career to work at home, raising her family. Bernadette also volunteered numerous hours both inside and outside our church, caring for others. Her two boys were just teenagers when she developed cancer.

Both before and after her diagnosis, she had a strong, positive faith; throughout her treatment, she prayed for a cure and she believed she would receive one. We prayed together. Bernadette died within two years of the discovery of her tumor.

There had been no miracle cure for Bernadette, though we prayed, though we passionately believed. My faith staggered at her death, then reeled again from the discovery of a tumor of my own. I realized, that for all my ministering, mine had been but a nodding acquaintance with death. Now death and I had an intimate relationship, and I was afraid. I prayed for help, and yet, so had Bernadette. If Christ is the Great Physician, where is he? If God says to us, "Ask and you shall receive," and promises, "Lo, I am with you always," how do we explain that some people are never cured? That they die? What good are our prayers for healing?

While restored health is not always the outcome, I know now that the prayers themselves are invaluable. I have a friend, Connie Wintler, who first battled breast cancer in 1967. With no alternatives to radical surgery and with a public that kept a muzzle on discussing anything so acutely personal, Connie found herself wandering through a marshland of fear. Her spiritual focus was the Lord's Prayer, which she prayed repeatedly. "I thought I was going to die and I was figuring, figuring," says Connie. "Who could I get to marry my husband and take care of my kids? One of my sisters? I had myself toes-pointed-up for a long time."

There was no miracle cure, nor was there a funeral. Surgeons removed her breast. Then late one night, just after surgery, she suddenly found herself wide awake and watching as a dark rectangle formed on the ceiling. Later, friends would speculate that she simply came to grips with mortality, but at that moment all Connie knew was that dark spot held not fear, but only peace and comfort, and she slipped into deep, relaxing sleep.

Connie's battles with cancer are still not over. She fought it again in 1984, and recently underwent surgery for a tumor lodged next to her brain. Adversity has toughened her faith while not silencing her questions, which often still center on prayers that are not answered—"Or at least, not answered the way I want," she says. But since that night in 1967, her outlook on life and on death has decidedly changed. She can make rational decisions about her medical treatments, make in-the-event-of-death plans and go about leading her life. Her prayers have not forever cured her, but Connie has, in a large sense, been healed. She is not afraid.

To be healed and to be cured can mean different things, even in the Bible. What we translate in English as "healing," in Greek appears as *sozo*, literally "to make whole"—a concept quite different from being made well. Through prayer, Connie is whole. Her faith is not tattered, her life is not a wreck.

If prayers can cause that, I need it. I need to feel at peace with whatever the future might hold. I need to feel somewhat in control of my medical care and I need to feel whole.

You may be in a physical crisis for which doctors have no cure and pretending that death doesn't exist would be ludicrous. Praying may not cure you. Still, to pray for health even in the face of unavoidable death is absolutely valid. For whatever the physical outcome, your prayers will deepen your relationship with God and produce an unexpected healing: a mind more capable of making sound decisions and a peace that recognizes life beyond death. If you know your designer and are living as you were designed, the eventual demise of your body will not destroy you. You possess a health that transcends the death of your body.

As Christians, we call this wholeness that transcends death "salvation." Through our relationship with God, we are saved from death. Once we pass from life to more life, the apostle Paul tells us that a spiritual body—related to but different from the old physical body—will be designed to shelter the life God has given to each and every human being:

> Someone will ask, "How can the dead be raised to life? What kind of body will they have?" You fool! When you plant a seed in the ground, it does not sprout to life unless it dies. And what you plant is a bare seed, perhaps a grain of wheat or some other grain, not the full-bodied plant that will later grow up. God provides that seed with the body he wishes; he gives each seed its own proper body. . . . This is how it will be when the dead are raised to life. When the body is buried, it is mortal; when raised, it will be immortal. When buried, it is ugly and weak; when raised, it will be beautiful and strong. When buried, it is a physical body; when raised, it will be a spiritual body.
>
> —I CORINTHIANS 15:35–38, 42–44

What that spiritual body will be like is a mystery that someday we will all understand in greater detail. For the moment, all we need to know is that death is not the end. And if death is not the end, what have we to fear?

In 1987, Henri Nouwen—priest, author, and man of faith—was struck in the back by the protruding mirror of a passing truck as he walked along the edge of a roadway near Toronto, Canada. A ruptured spleen brought him to the brink of death. His near-death experience he described as walking through a sea whose waves had been rolled away, protected as he moved to the other shore. And he experienced a very personal, gentle, nonjudgmental presence:

"It was not a warm light, a rainbow, or an open door that I *saw*, but a human yet divine presence that I felt . . . My whole life had been an arduous attempt to follow Jesus . . . Jesus had been very close, but also very distant; a friend, but also a stranger, a source of hope, but also of fear, guilt, and shame. But now, when I walked around the portal of death, all ambiguity was gone. He was there, the Lord of my life, saying, "Come to me, come."[1]

For Nouwen, death lost its fearful power in the face of God's unconditional love. Waking from a life-saving operation, he had an immediate sense of being sent to make that all-embracing love known to all people. After his recovery, Nouwen continued to write and lecture until his death from a heart attack in September 1997.

Experiencing this magnificent sense of God is the value of our prayers: In praying, we open our lives to God, inviting God to work with us. In a relationship with God we find healing and hope, and we can make our plans and choose our paths, without fear of death.

That is not to say there is no grief. Pastor and theologian Carlisle Marny has said all our grief comes from the fact that something ends before we are ready for it to end. Even when death is expected, we are frequently not prepared. My grandmother was ninety-four when she died and despite her advanced age and obviously frail condition I experienced an enormous sense of loss. She had suffered strokes and was confined to a convalescent hospital. She said she was tired of her body and ready to die: Her normal functions had deteriorated, she had to be diapered, and moving her caused brittle bones to break. Yet, when she finally died, it spun me around. I wept. Her body was gone, I would not be able to go talk to her anymore, I would not see her smile. She would never use those loving, wrinkled hands to bake cinnamon rolls again. There would be a hole in my life. She was *my* grandmother.

Death of the body brings with it emotional pain and loss. Met with the news of Lazarus' death, even Jesus grieved. Pause for a moment now to observe Jesus in the passage from John on the following page. Imagine the feelings that generated Jesus' emotional response.

[1] Henri Nouwen expanded this in *Beyond the Mirror: Reflections on Death and Life*, by Henri J. M. Nouwen, Crossroad Publishing Company, New York, 1991.

Invite God to work with you. Using Imaginative Prayer (page 44), let
this story of Jesus and the death of a friend come alive in your mind.

MEDITATION ON JESUS AND DEATH

Mary arrived where Jesus was, and as soon as she saw him, she fell at his feet. "LORD," she said, "if you had been here, my brother would not have died!"

Jesus saw her weeping, and he saw how the people with her were weeping also; his heart was touched, and he was deeply moved. "Where have you buried him?" he asked them.

"Come and see, LORD," they answered.

Jesus wept. "See how much he loved him!" the people said.

But some of them said, "He gave sight to the blind man, didn't he? Could he not have kept Lazarus from dying?"

—JOHN 11:32–37

Now read and remember.

INVITATION TO BELIEVE

Jesus said to her, "I am the resurrection and the life. Those who believe in me will live, even though they die; and those who live and believe in me will never die. Do you believe this?"

—JOHN 11:25–26

At the time of my diagnosis, it was the impending loss of my own life that I was grieving. I was slipping and stumbling in my journey through the valley, and it took both the 23rd Psalm and Paul's teachings to help me regain my balance. But finally I heard the words of God.

In Psalm 23, the psalmist calls death a *shadow*, an interruption of light that has no reality of its own. If the light source was the radiance of God's divine love, what was blocking the light? What was making death seem so dark, real? Fear.

During those first days after diagnosis, my fear blocked the warmth of God's love from shining into my life. My fear created the shadows and gave death its substance. I felt too young; I was not ready to die. I had too much to do still; I didn't want to die. I had responsibilities; I couldn't die! My preoccupation with that fear stopped me from seeing the truth: Death has no substance. When the body dies, the being still exists.

People are aware of this possibility, as evidenced in the everyday language we all use. We say, "He *has* a great body"; we don't say, "He *is* a great body." Or we hear someone say, "Wow, what a body she has." We don't hear, "What a body she is." What is it, then, that has the body?

What has the body is the being, the "spirit"—in Hebrew *rauch*, in Greek *pneuma*, both meaning "breath" or "wind." Paul teaches that the body is a tool given to the being to use for a period of time. My grandmother's being was strong; her body was spent, and when her body died, the "breath" was gone. Her being no longer needed her body.

It is that spirit, that being which makes the body lovable, that makes it something more than just a bag of bones. Human beings don't generally love dead bodies—what we love is the being that energizes the body, that gives the body warmth and humor, that makes the body interesting and a joy to be around. The death of a body is a loss, but the ultimate nature of that loss, as Paul says, is an illusion, because the being or spirit which energized the body still exists. Read for yourself Paul's teachings on the following page.

Use Divine Reading (page 29) to hear God's words for you.

BEING AND BODY

Even though our physical being is gradually decaying, yet our spiritual being is renewed day after day. And this small and temporary trouble we suffer will bring us a tremendous and eternal glory, much greater than the trouble.

For we fix our attention not on things that are seen, but on things that are unseen. What can be seen lasts only for a time, but what cannot be seen lasts forever.

For we know that when this tent we live in—our body here on earth—is torn down, God will have a house in heaven for us to live in, a home he himself has made, which will last forever.

—2 CORINTHIANS 4:16–5:1

If God has designed us with bodies that will ultimately die, then why should we be uncomfortable and even frightened at the prospect of our own deaths? We affirm in our holidays that God has something more in store for us. Easter week centers on the crucifixion and death is acknowledged as inevitable, but the real focus is on resurrection. Death is not the end, merely the transition, the passageway to more life. Each human is born with a body designed by God to house a being filled with life, a being created in the image of God. That being will energize the body it is given, use it, enjoy it, coach it through physical illnesses, and eventually discard it. And as our bodies go from birth to death, our beings go from less life to more life. The beings, at least those who open themselves to a relationship with God, continue to expand.

Instead of fearing evil, we can trust the God who comes to us, and keeps coming after our bodies are gone. In life and in death I do belong to God. After the shock of my diagnosis it took many intense journeys into meditation to reach this place of peace, but at last there came a night when I went to bed calm. Since then, over and over I focused on that phrase: in life and in death . . . Over and over, I have felt the reassurance that whatever the future held for me—life or death—God has something better planned for me than I could possibly plan myself. Today I still fear the unknown (What will death be like? Will it hurt?), but I do not see death as evil.

Instead, when the moment of death comes, I anticipate it will be filled with the kind of fear that accompanies all new adventures. I imagine it will be somewhat like what I felt when friends first took me to the top of the Cornice, one of the highest ski runs in California. The sight was both beautiful and terrifying. The run itself was invisible because of the lip of snow protruding out from the mountain. I wanted to make the run, yet I was petrified at the same time. Then the moment came when I slipped over the lip of that mountaintop and I was committed—terrified, excited, and committed. By the time it was over it had been one of the most exhilarating experiences I had ever known.

I believe that the experience of death will bring much the same feeling. Through meditation, the wall of fear that blocked the light has been removed, and the brilliance of God's love eradicates the shadow of death. The shadow gone, I can see clearly that I have a future; and with that clear vision comes a hope and a confidence that let me live with joy here and now.

Use Divine Reading (page 29) to let these words illuminate your heart.

VICTORY OVER DEATH

In view of all this, what can we say? If God is for us, who can be against us? Certainly not God, who did not even keep back his own Son, but offered him for us all! He gave us his Son—will he not also freely give us all things? . . . Who, then, can separate us from the love of Christ? Can trouble do it, or hardship or persecution or hunger or poverty or danger or death? . . .

No, in all these things we have complete victory through him who loved us! For I am certain that nothing can separate us from his love: neither death nor life, neither angels nor other heavenly rulers or powers, neither the present nor the future, neither the world above nor the world below—there is nothing in all creation that will ever be able to separate us from the love of God which is ours through Christ Jesus our Lord.

—ROMANS 8:31–32, 35, 37–39

REFLECTIONS

Use Divine Reading (page 29) to remember this promise from Jesus.

PROMISE OF A FUTURE

"Do not be worried and upset," Jesus told them. "Believe in God and believe also in me. There are many rooms in my Father's house, and I am going to prepare a place for you. I would not tell you this if it were not so. And after I go and prepare a place for you, I will come back and take you to myself, so that you will be where I am. You know the way that leads to the place where I am going."

Thomas said to him, "LORD, we do not know where you are going; so how can we know the way to get there?"

Jesus answered him, "I am the way, the truth, and the life."

—JOHN 14:1–6A

REFLECTIONS

Use Divine Reading (page 29) to explore this promise.

PROMISE OF A NEW CREATION

Then I saw a new heaven and a new earth. The first heaven and the first earth disappeared, and the sea vanished. And I saw the Holy City, the new Jerusalem, coming down out of heaven from God, prepared and ready, like a bride dressed to meet her husband. I heard a loud voice speaking from the throne: "Now God's home is with people! He will live with them, and they shall be his people. God himself will be with them, and he will be their God. He will wipe away all tears from their eyes. There will be no more death, no more crying or pain. The old things have disappeared."

Then the one who sits on the throne said, "And now I make all things new!" He also said to me, "Write this, because these words are true and can be trusted."

—REVELATION 21:1–5

REFLECTIONS

Simply read and remember.

YOU BELONG

We do not live for ourselves only, and we do not die for ourselves only. If we live, it is for the LORD that we live, and if we die, it is for the LORD that we die. So whether we live or die, we belong to the LORD. For Christ died and rose to life in order to be the LORD of the living and of the dead.

—ROMANS 14:7–9

REFLECTIONS

Before going on to Chapter 7, make my prayer your own.

Your Will Be Done

I don't like what is happening to me, O God.
I wish this were not happening to me.
Get this out of my life.
Nevertheless, I trust you. You love me.
You have demonstrated that
over and over.
You love me more even than I love myself.
I do trust you.
I trust that what you have in store for me
is better and more life-giving than
anything I could have planned for
myself.
So, your will be done, O God.
And let's get on with it.

7.

DESIGNED FOR LIFE

———————————————— ■ ————————————————

Don't you know that your body is the temple of the Holy Spirit,
who lives in you and who was given to you by God?

—1 CORINTHIANS 6:19

After the avalanche of emotions, after the bewilderment, the anger, and the fear, I arrived at last where I had begun: in a body with cancer.

Now, however, things seemed different. While physically I was in the same dire situation, my fear was gone. And my approach to my illness was changing as I internalized three basic truths.

The first truth was that my body had been designed to physically cure itself. In nearly fifty years of living, my body had grown and changed, and occasionally fallen ill, but on the whole it had done a superb job of healing itself with very little help from anybody. By design a tiny baby changes into a full-grown adult. By design, small teeth fall out and new ones come in, old cells die and new ones take their place. Our bodies are not created in some random, haphazard way. They are designed as vessels for life.

A tape by surgeon Bernie S. Siegel brought this concept home to me, and none too soon. It was a crucial time. With a week to go before my radical prostatectomy and in a state of near panic, I found myself driving up the California coast, back to the Jesuit Retreat Center I had visited just that summer. Along the way, I slipped *Getting Ready: Meditations for Surgery, Chemo and Radiation* into the tape deck. In the midst of discussions on how to prepare for medical intervention, Dr. Siegel comments that the body is the greatest healing mechanism in the universe. Doctors don't heal you; they merely assist the body in its own natural process.

All of which triggered the second truth: I am more than simply a body.

Human beings are the pinnacle of God's creation. We are all miraculous in design, and we are more than bodies. God designed the human body to house the being, and it is the being that is created in the image of God. At age seventy-eight, Buckminster Fuller, in a 1973 *Saturday Review*, described in a playful way this same truth:

> I am 78 years old, and at my age I find that I have now taken in more than 1,000 tons of water, food and air, the chemistry of which is temporarily employed for different lengths of time as hair, skin, flesh, bones and blood, etc., then progressively discarded. I weighed in at seven pounds, and I went on to 70, then 170 and even 207 pounds. And then I lost 70 pounds, and I said, "who was that 70 pounds?" because here I am. The 70 pounds I got rid of was 10 times the flesh-and-bone inventory at which I had weighed in, in 1895. This lost 70 pounds of organic chemistry obviously wasn't me. We have been making a great error in

identifying me and you as these truly sensorial passing chemistries.[1]

Facing a terrifying diagnosis, I found it invaluable to remember that I am a being who inhabits a body. Someday this body, this passing chemistry will die—it is not designed to last forever. But I am *a being* who has a body.

So, while my body had cancer, *I* did not. My being was not sick; my *body* was sick. Armed with that knowledge, I was finally able to step back and see the larger picture. I realized the third truth: My being could work with the magnificently complex instrument God had designed.

This third realization let me take charge of my own medical treatment. My mind didn't have cancer, it could take in data and process it. My mind could still make decisions about what kind of treatment I wanted, who I wanted to do the treatment, and when I wanted to have the treatment done. I felt a tremendous liberation when I once again realized that I was still free to make choices about my own body and my future. I could take responsibility for my own cure.

My friend and fellow pastor James C. Huffstutler has preached this "take charge" philosophy for years, having faced down what seemed like a never-ending onslaught of dreadful health problems. He was just in his mid-twenties in 1964 when he started having seizures and finally blacked out in his apartment.

"I didn't know what a seizure was," James says. "These crazy things started happening when I had the flu, and I thought, 'This is the worst flu I ever had.' "

What James actually had was a massive, benign brain tumor. Surgery to remove it went well. He traveled the next year on a fellowship to Scotland, where wintry cobblestone streets took the blame

[1] Courtesy Buckminster Fuller Institute, Santa Barbara, CA.

for his increasingly difficult time walking. But when James returned to the States in 1966, his brain surgeon instantly diagnosed another huge tumor. This one required two surgeries, adding up to three brain surgeries in as many years. The whole experience left him with loss of flexion on both sides of his body. However, putting things into perspective, James didn't see the loss as much of a problem. "I carried on pretty naturally with a cane," he says. "I was never going to be a ballet dancer anyway."

That wasn't the end of James's troubles, though. A heart attack hit him in his mid-thirties and a pacemaker was installed. Nevertheless, James married and had two children. Then, in 1990, when the children were about six and seven years old, James noticed his vision was deteriorating, the result of yet another brain tumor. Because of the pacemaker, surgeons refused to operate.

"I tell my parishioners, 'This is your life, you need to stay in charge of it. Work with physicians, but don't hand it over,'" says James. But after all that preaching, he didn't follow his own advice. "I just accepted an inevitable decline to death. With blindness coming on, I was trying to figure out how many more years I could work to put some money in the bank for my two little kids. How guilty I felt, having fathered these children only to leave them with nothing."

Luckily, his parishioners themselves intervened, among them James's cardiologist and the cardiologist's wife, an oncologist, who together campaigned successfully for a fourth brain surgery. The tumor was removed and the progression toward blindness stopped. James's vision is still hampered and though a rainy-day fall broke his leg and moved him onto two walking canes, he is mentally ready for whatever the future holds. "I may need to learn some new skills, but what's new?" Meanwhile, he says, "If you ever need to talk to the tumor king, I'm here."

The being that inhabits our bodies has tremendous power and is quite capable of promoting a successful treatment program even before the program begins. Years ago I remember reading Maxwell

Maltz's *Psychocybernetics*, a study about the power of the mind to influence the body. Three groups of people were recruited to shoot basketball free throws. Each group was to be tested twice, thirty days apart. In between each test the first group did not practice free throws and the second practiced fifteen minutes per day. The third, for fifteen minutes every day, simply imagined in detail shooting free throws. Thirty days later, group number one had made no improvement. And while group two had made significant gains, the people in group three had improved nearly as much using just their minds.

Pause for a moment now, and remember Paul's teachings on the power of the mind.

Use Divine Reading (page 29) to remember Paul's teachings.

The Power of the Mind

Do not conform yourselves to the standards of this world, but let God transform you inwardly by a complete change of your mind. Then you will be able to know the will of God—what is good and is pleasing to him and is perfect.

—ROMANS 12:2

REFLECTIONS

A wealth of studies have expanded on the power of the mind, and many fields have applied the findings. If you have watched the Winter Olympics, you have probably seen downhill skiers using mental imaging. At the top of the run, eyes closed, they envision the entire course before they take off, their muscles responding to each turn.

Applying the concept to myself, then, it made sense that visualizing my coming surgery and all else to follow could literally prepare my body to participate in the treatment, not just endure the ordeal. With imaging, I could have a dozen successful cancer surgeries before ever entering the operating room.

More, I could combine imaging with prayer. Though I needed no empirical evidence to convince me to pray, the scientific community's examination of healing prayer has been extensively chronicled by Larry Dossey, M.D. Dossey's ten-year compilation of double- and triple-blind laboratory experiments and case histories traces the effect of concentrated prayer on human subjects as well as documenting the reaction in specific bacterial cultures and flasks of cancer cells. So powerful were the statistical results, that Dossey concluded the use of prayer will eventually be fully incorporated into mainstream medical care—pervasive to the point that not to recommend the use of prayer "will one day constitute medical malpractice."[2]

So, with time running short, I decided not only to visualize surgery, but to incorporate prayerful meditation and invite God to be present. I started immediately with three healing meditations a day. Using Imaginative Prayer, I began each meditation with a prayer of preparation, and then stated my desire—usually to have a deeper knowledge of God's healing power. Then in place of meditating on Scripture, I mentally encouraged the different parts of my body to cooperate with the surgeon in ridding my body of cancer.

[2] *Healing Words: The Power of Prayer and the Practice of Medicine,* by Larry Dossey, M.D. HarperSanFrancisco, 1993.

I talked to my body, saying things like "Prostate, I want you to hold on to that tumor. You don't have to fight it. You don't have to kill it. Just don't let any of it get away. In a few days my body and I are going to ask you to give up your life for the good of the body as a whole. There is nothing greater one life form can do for another than to willingly give up life for the greater good of all."

To the blood vessels, I said, "Channel our blood away from the tumor. Don't give it any more nourishment! And when our surgeon comes into us, cooperate with him—he is our friend, after all. Open up and let him through; then close up quickly so we don't lose a lot of blood."

The muscles I pictured as hands joined together across the center aisle of our church sanctuary, letting go of one another as my physician came in and rejoining after he passed by. And to the nerves I said, "I want you to get as far away from the prostate as you possibly can." (Any man facing prostate surgery will appreciate the nuances of that.) The image I saw in my mind was of a grade school disaster drill and the nerves plastering themselves against the far wall. Throughout all this, I pictured each body part silently saying, "Yes."

It was late evening on the second day of these meditations when something most unexpected occurred.

I was meditating as usual, previewing my successful surgery. I had the thought that my doctor ought to know that my body and I were prepared . . . perhaps, since I would be unconscious, he could talk to the different parts of my body during surgery and tell them what he wanted them to do. So in my mind I pictured leaving my body—already being prepped on the operating table—and I mentally found the surgeon in an adjoining room. I was just about to make my request when I realized if he did not normally talk to bodies in the operating room (probably a fairly safe assumption), others might think he was losing touch with reality and haul him away before he had even finished the operation.

Abandoning that line of thought, I chose instead to mentally move back into the operating room and view my body from above. My body was now surrounded by the entire medical team. As the team operated, I watched. Then suddenly, I was no longer in control of my meditation. To my astonishment, Jesus appeared in the operating room.

He was standing in the back corner, also watching the operation. He spoke to me, not to my body lying on the table, saying, "Charles, while you are unconscious I will take care of your body. After all, it is not your body, it is mine. You have given it to me. It is my body, and my body has already been broken for you."

I cannot tell you how long the experience lasted, nor can I truly describe the relief and peace that came to me from that moment on. According to my journal I prayed, "Lord, Lord, forgive me when my own fears and concerns cause me to forget that I am yours . . . that you care more about me than I care about myself. I do love you. I do trust you."

I was about to say the Lord's Prayer when impulsively I added:

"One more thing, Lord, just for my information: I have been through a lot the last few weeks, I've come to you every day in prayer and meditation, and I haven't heard anything from you since the Monday before Thanksgiving when I was on the plane to Oregon. It has been a hellish two months. Where have you been?"

I felt Jesus smile and I heard him say with more love than words can convey, "Charles, Charles, I was always with you."

The message I received during that meditation was not for me alone; it is for all people of faith. When you accept Christ, you give your "whole self to his service," including your body. God in Christ cares for every human being and gave his body to be broken for all. Whether we are aware of it or not, the God who comes to us in Christ is present with each of us in whatever treatment program we choose. We are not alone in our journey through the valley of shadows.

Take a few minutes to reflect on the unique and wondrous nature of the place God has given you in creation. Use Divine Reading (page 29) to let these words lift your spirit.

MEDITATION ON HUMAN DESIGN

O LORD, our LORD,
Your greatness is seen in all
the world! . . .

When I look at the sky, which you
have made,
at the moon and the stars,
which you set in their
places—
what are human beings, that you
think of them;
mere mortals, that you care for
them?

Yet you have made them inferior only to
yourself;
you crowned them with glory
and honor.

—PSALMS 8:1–5

Use Divine Reading (page 29) as you read and remember.

CHRIST'S GIFT

[Jesus] took a piece of bread, gave thanks to God, broke it, and gave it to them, saying, "This is my body, which is given for you. Do this in memory of me." In the same way, he gave them the cup after the supper, saying, "This cup is God's new covenant sealed with my blood, which is poured out for you."

—LUKE 22:19–20

GOD'S DESIRE

For God loved the world so much that he gave his only Son, so that everyone who believes in him may not die but have eternal life. For God did not send his Son into the world to be its judge, but to be its savior.

—JOHN 3:16–17

Reflect on this story of healing. Using Imaginative Prayer (page 44),
picture the man who had been in physical crisis for thirty-eight years.
Observe Jesus walking through the crowd, and imagine the look on his
face as he encounters the sick man. Listen to Jesus' question: "Do you
want to get well?" Let that become a question to you.
What is your response?

DESIRE FOR HEALING

After this, Jesus went to Jerusalem for a religious festival. Near the Sheep Gate in Jerusalem there is a pool with five porches; in Hebrew it is called Bethzatha. A large crowd of sick people were lying on the porches—the blind, the lame, and the paralyzed. A man was there who had been sick for thirty-eight years. Jesus saw him lying there, and he knew that the man had been sick for such a long time; so he asked him, "Do you want to get well?"

The sick man answered, "Sir, I don't have anyone here to put me in the pool when the water is stirred up; while I am trying to get in, somebody else gets there first."

Jesus said to him, "Get up, pick up your mat, and walk." Immediately the man got well; he picked up his mat and started walking.

—JOHN 5:1–9

As you read through this collection of healing stories observe the desire of Christ to restore health. Observe the importance of the faith of the person seeking healing. Take time to use either Divine Reading (page 29), Imaginative Prayer (page 44), or both on any of these passages.

FAITH AND HEALING

As Jesus went along, the people were crowding him from every side. Among them was a woman who had suffered from severe bleeding for twelve years; she had spent all she had on doctors, but no one had been able to cure her. She came up in the crowd behind Jesus and touched the edge of his cloak, and her bleeding stopped at once. Jesus asked, "Who touched me?"

Everyone denied it, and Peter said, "Master, the people are all around you and crowding in on you."

But Jesus said, "Someone touched me, for I knew it when power went out of me." The woman saw that she had been found out, so she came trembling and threw herself at Jesus' feet. There in front of everybody, she told him why she had touched him and how she had been healed at once. Jesus said to her, "My daughter, your faith has made you well. Go in peace."

—LUKE 8:42–48

REFLECTIONS

HEALING OF A DISTURBED MAN

As soon as Jesus got out of the boat, he was met by a man who came out of the burial caves there. This man had an evil spirit in him and lived among the tombs. Nobody could keep him tied with chains any more; many times his feet and his hands had been tied, but every time he broke the chains and smashed the irons on his feet. He was too strong for anyone to control him. Day and night he wandered among the tombs and through the hills, screaming and cutting himself with stones.

He was some distance away when he saw Jesus; so he ran, fell on his knees before him, and screamed in a loud voice, "Jesus, Son of the most high God! What do you want with me for God's sake, I beg you, don't punish me!" (He said this because Jesus was saying, "Evil spirit, come out of this man!")

So Jesus asked him, "What is your name?" The man answered, "My name is 'Mob'—there are so many of us!" and he kept begging Jesus not to send the evil spirits out of that region.

There was a large herd of pigs near by, feeding on a hillside. So the spirits begged Jesus, "Send us to the pigs, and let us go into them." He let them go, and the evil spirits went out of the man and entered the pigs. The whole herd—about two thousand pigs in all—rushed down the side of the cliff into the lake and was drowned.

The men who had been taking care of the pigs ran away and spread the news in the town and among the farms. People went out to see what had happened, and when they came to Jesus, they saw the man who used to have the mob of demons in him. He was sitting there, clothed and in his right mind; and they were all afraid. Those who had seen it told the people what had happened to the man with the demons, and about the pigs.

So they asked Jesus to leave their territory.

As Jesus was getting into the boat, the man who had had the demons begged him, "Let me go with you!"

But Jesus would not let him. Instead, he told him, "Go back home to your family and tell them how much the Lord has done for you and how kind he has been to you."

So the man left and went all through the Ten Towns, telling what Jesus had done for him. And all who heard it were amazed.

—MARK 5:2–20

HEALING AND FAITH

When Jesus had finished saying all these things to the people, he went to Capernaum. A Roman officer there had a servant who was very dear to him; the man was sick and about to die. When the officer heard about Jesus, he sent some Jewish elders to ask him to come and heal his servant. They came to Jesus and begged him earnestly, "This man really deserves your help. He loves our people and he himself built a synagogue for us."

So Jesus went with them. He was not far from the house when the officer sent friends to tell him, "Sir, don't trouble yourself. I do not deserve to have you come into my house, neither do I consider myself worthy to come to you in person. Just give the order, and my servant will get well. I, too, am a man placed under the authority of superior officers, and I have soldiers under me. I order this one, 'Go!' and he goes; I order that one, 'Come!' and he comes; and I order my slave, 'Do this!' and he does it."

Jesus was surprised when he heard this; he turned around and said to the crowd following him, "I tell you, I have never found faith like this, not even in Israel!"

The messengers went back to the officer's house and found his servant well.

—LUKE 7:1–10

The Power of Faith

They came to Jericho, and as Jesus was leaving with his disciples and a large crowd, a blind beggar named Bartimaeus son of Timaeus was sitting by the road. When he heard that it was Jesus of Nazareth, he began to shout, "Jesus! Son of David! Have mercy on me!"

Many of the people scolded him and told him to be quiet. But he shouted even more loudly, "Son of David, have mercy on me!"

Jesus stopped and said, "Call him."

So they called the blind man. "Cheer up!" they said. "Get up, he is calling you."

So he threw off his cloak, jumped up, and came to Jesus.

"What do you want me to do for you?" Jesus asked him.

"Teacher," the blind man answered, "I want to see again."

"Go," Jesus told him, "your faith has made you well."

At once he was able to see and followed Jesus on the road.

—MARK 10:46–52

8.

HELPERS IN HEALING

∎

I found myself earnestly explaining to the young minister that I did not believe in God, "but I've discovered that I can't live as though I didn't believe in him."

—MADELEINE L'ENGLE, *A CIRCLE OF QUIET*

I have a number of friends who are "private" people; they keep their illnesses to themselves. While I respect their opinion, I do not share it. For years I have observed the powerful response of communities—church communities and other support groups—that rally around a person in need and become prime players in creating both healing and wholeness. When my own crisis came, I remembered the words of Jesus, "You shall know the truth and the truth shall set you free" (John 8:2). I chose to make my information public, and my illness was announced in Sunday worship one week after diagnosis.

Multiple benefits came from my openness about a disease that is not generally discussed. People volunteered names of talented local physicians, forwarded medical articles, and passed along other sources of information. As a result of the Sunday announcement, I can name over a dozen men in our church alone who have now had their first PSA tests. One is now being treated for prostate cancer. My candor has also opened the door for others to discuss past illnesses: I discovered the congregation I had served for over twelve years was filled with cancer survivors, many of them younger than I.

I do not for a moment regret going public. Bodies are designed to need other bodies. Only when one body is united with another body can human life be perpetuated. Even with today's miracle of artificial insemination, life comes only from the joining of one body with another. Bodies are designed to need bodies in order to survive.

In the same way, beings are designed to be with other beings. Our very understanding of a God as Trinity recognizes that divine nature is one of community, a fellowship of love from which all life flows. As beings created in the image of God, we are designed for relationship with others.

Immediate family in this instance is not enough. In catastrophic illness, as hospital personnel will attest, our family members are rarely capable of providing all the emotional support we need. They are often swamped by their own concerns for the future or occasionally waylaid by fear and misunderstanding of the disease itself. They may need to be taken care of at the very time they are called on to be caretakers.

So it is helpful to be a part of a larger community of love. And, just as your chosen community will be of immense help to you, it will also offer its wealth of resources to your blood family. Even for the closest of families, struggling through a health crisis and its aftermath is a daunting process. My daughters remember well the night I broke the news. For Elizabeth, age twelve, the announcement triggered a major move away from childhood priorities and into the beginnings of adult perspective. "You were driving us home from gymnastics and you asked if we wanted to go to Santa Barbara that weekend," she recalls. "We told you no, because we had all these other plans. After dinner, after you told us you were sick, we decided we'd all better go to Santa Barbara."

For Sarah, one year older, comfort had to be found away from the family dinner table: "I'm not one to show any emotions in front of other people," she says. "So I went into my room and started to cry. I called my friend to tell her the news and tell her she couldn't sleep over on Friday. At first, she didn't believe me that you had cancer. She thought I was joking."

My daughters turned for help to our church's associate pastors. Church members drove my girls to their appointments when my wife could not and tried to field questions as best they could. Mirroring my own forthrightness, my family felt free to turn to their own friends, and find comfort there. Illness is not an experience of an individual alone and when it is conscious decision that determines whether we go public or not, I advocate finding a church community or support group, putting trust in its people and its resources, and speaking out.

In some illnesses, though, the onset is so sudden and the symptoms so severe there is no time for well-thought-out announcements. For Sally Anderson, the lack of initial outside contact and the subsequent isolation were devastating:

"It was the middle of the night. I remember I got up to go to the bathroom and came back to bed, when all of a sudden, my body didn't work. My right leg and my arm just cramped up. I fell to my left, but I managed to get back on the bed and crawl under the covers.

"My husband, Lance, said I looked 'funny.' I remember him going through the phone book, looking for the obstetrician. He carried me downstairs, put me in the car, and drove fast. The only thing that bothered me at the time was that my hand was all shriveled up."

Sally was in her mid-thirties and exactly three months pregnant when an undetected hole in her heart triggered a stroke in the middle of the night. In her crisis, two lives were at stake. Here is her description of the moment when just the first of the lasting repercussions raised its head:

"You still think you're speaking intelligently. I was in the hospital, trying to tell my sister to cancel some family pictures so we could get our deposit back. I kept telling her and she would just stare at me. It made me so mad; I thought, 'Why won't she just do it?' Then it dawned on me nobody could understand what I was saying.

"I found out later what was coming out was '007, 008, mister and missus'—over and over. A woman came into my room and said, 'Mrs. Anderson, this is a chicken; can you say chicken?' Lance was furious. He shouted, 'She can't even say her own name!' He was scared. Later, he said he would have done anything to keep me alive."

Five months later, Sally had only partially recovered. Doctors took Sally's baby by cesarean section. Her son, Christopher, was born with neurological damage.

"I stopped breathing three or four times during the operation, and the doctor kept slapping me across the face, saying, 'Breathe!' I said, 'I am!' She said, 'No, you're not!' Then the nurses whisked the baby out to another room—I didn't even get to see him. The doctor said, 'Can this mother kiss her son?' They brought him back and let me kiss him."

At home with her baby, exhausted and embarrassed at being unable to communicate, Sally could not bring herself to reach out for help from her church family:

"I wanted to go to church so much, but I just couldn't. People would have asked how I was, and I wouldn't even have been able to speak to them. I didn't want people to see me that way. I remember I sat here on the hillside above our house, looking down at our church on the street below, and crying."

With all its shortcomings, with all the human weaknesses so evident, the community of faith is still one of the major divine channels through which God comes to us. A woman suffering from

Crohn's disease, Sara Jackson, literally collapsed in front of a church—our church, in fact. For better or worse, from that moment on isolation was impossible. Our faith community was instantly involved and Sara couldn't have avoided our help had she wanted to. She and her family later officially joined our congregation. Here is her story:

"At first, I thought I had some kind of a bug.

"I was five months pregnant with my first child when we went vacationing in Mexico and I came home with what I thought was dysentery. The doctors speculated it was an inflammation and eventually the symptoms went away. When I was five months pregnant with my second child, the same symptoms appeared. Initially, I didn't think about it. I was just too busy—you know how it is when you are raising kids.

"We went to Eleuthra and again I thought I had eaten something bad. But this time, when we got home I was really sick. I was diagnosed with Crohn's disease, an embarrassing, autoimmune disease where among other things, you lose control of your bowels. I was bedridden for six months."

Then one morning, Sara decided she had had enough inactivity. A neighbor had involved Sara's boys in a local church Bible camp and though her blood count was shockingly low, Sara was determined to get reinvolved in her sons' lives.

"I had lost so much blood that I saw stars when I got out of bed in the morning. But I really wanted to help this camp—if only to buy snacks. My husband said to me that morning before he left for work, 'Now, you're not going to do anything crazy, are you?' I said, 'Oh, no, just cookies.' "

Sara drove to the church, then walked across the street to a local grocery and bought the snacks. As simple as the task sounds, physically it was more than her body could take.

"I was standing in front of the market, waiting for the traffic light to change, when I knew I had to sit down right then. Next thing I knew, I was lying on the sidewalk.

"The box boys came over and said, 'Are you all right?' I said, 'Yep, I just need to get these cookies to the church.' They said, 'Sit here, we'll call an ambulance.' But I said no—I couldn't just disappear, with my boys wondering where I had gone. I got up and started walking, but I made it only as far as across the street. There I passed out cold, right on the curb.

"A woman in the congregation ended up driving me to the hospital. I remember feeling embarrassed because I bled all over her car. I was given a list of twenty blood donors from the church and I used twelve of them. People from the church fed us. Our kids were taken care of. We weren't even members. It was a complete outpouring of love."

You have similar resources. If you are a church member, support is as close as your church phone directory. If you are not a member of a church, this is the time to get your courage up and call one. Start a relationship with a local congregation. The people there will serve you, too. Talk with the pastor. Let him or her advise you and pray with you. If you have a "chain of prayer" or prayer teams in your church, have them pray for you. Welcome your elders or deacons to visit you. Listen to the stories of fellow travelers who have also faced crises and survived. Take tips from others who have found strength in their faith. If for any reason a church family is not accessible to you, seek out support groups through local medical centers. Create for yourself an intentional family, a chosen community, a channel to open you to God's healing love.

Take some time to focus on your own sources of support. If you are involved in a church, picture the faces of the people in your congregation who are most encouraging. If you are not involved in a church, substitute your community of support—friends, neighbors, coworkers, a club or other organization. Remember encouragement you've received from them. Give thanks for them. Using the pattern of Divine Reading (page 29), read this passage. As you do, keep in mind the difference between "cure" and "heal." God ultimately heals all of us, whether we are cured or not.

CALLING ON THE COMMUNITY OF FAITH

Are any among you in trouble? They should pray. Are any among you happy? They should sing praises. Are any among you sick? They should send for the church elders, who will pray for them and rub olive oil on them in the name of the Lord. This prayer made in faith will heal the sick; the Lord will restore them to health. . . .

—JAMES 5:13–16

REFLECTIONS

Even if you have always considered yourself the private type, an objective look at your health crisis will reveal a time already filled with doctors, nurses, medical technicians and therapists, family, pastors, church members, friends, and neighbors. These people, professionals and nonprofessionals alike, have the power to offer tremendous resources to your recovery.

They also have the power to interfere, and that downside to sharing the news of your illness cannot be denied. John Kunz recalls vividly some of the comments people made in the months after the chiropractic accident triggered his wife's brain stem stroke:

"I had a man come up, point his finger at me, and say, 'You're the reason this happened to Sue.' I said, 'Excuse me?' He said, 'You don't have enough faith.' I almost grabbed him. I said, 'It isn't up to me and my faith. It's up to God.' People like that always have to have an excuse.

"A woman came to me and said, 'I know why this happened to Sue.' 'Oh yeah? Why?' 'Stress. It's the way you run your house. It's always in chaos. Your house is always noisy.' I said, 'What do you expect with a house with four kids who have friends? Everyone brings one friend and you've got eight. I have regular children. They move through in herds. That's not chaos. That's normal.' She said, 'Well, that's the reason she had a stroke.'

"Another man went to some conference, came back, and said, 'God revealed to me why Sue isn't healed.' 'Oh yeah?' 'Demon possession.' 'Oh? What do we do about it?' 'I could cast out the demons.' I looked him in the eye and said, 'All right. Let's go out to the house right now and you cast out those demons. And if she's not completely healed after you're through, you get a six-foot head start.' He decided not to do that. I said, 'Then get out of here with that nonsense.' "

At the same time, the help other people offered was invaluable. With Sue in a deep coma and the hospital sixty-five miles from home, friends lent John a mobile home, parking it in the hospital lot.

"Our whole community got involved," John says. Well-wishers filled up the hospital waiting rooms and stayed for days, one close friend keeping lists of who came and relaying messages to John. People took care of John and Sue's children then and in the months that followed. They drove, cooked food, ran errands, and prayed.

People, people, people—God consistently favors coming to the world through people. The mystery and the majesty of the church from Peter and Paul until this day is that the church is the "body of Christ" made up of *people*, beings created in the image of God. They are common garden-variety people who often disappoint us, make mistakes, and get in trouble, but people nonetheless, through whom God works.

In my own experience, I did not have to endure the kind of comments John received. On the other hand, along with a flood of helpful books and tapes, my public announcement brought all sorts of bizarre advice, in particular articles on miracle drugs not approved for distribution in the United States. I was directed to special diets which may or may not have been helpful to my health; the most humorous for me was via a neighbor who was convinced that I could eradicate cancer from my body if I would only drink wheat grass juice daily for a week. The pungent taste of fresh grass made it hard for me not to moo like a cow.

I was directed to faith healers who had been helpful to one of my friends or someone they knew, though I had already chosen to trust in the God who heals and the gifted medical personnel through whom God most often works. So while some suggestions were undoubtedly helpful, many were not. Yet all were offered in a spirit of caring and genuine concern. When I could focus on the caring behind them, even the bizarre and totally useless gifts became a source of God working in my life to make me whole. My being was fed by the love of others.

A final benefit to announcing my diagnosis was that accurate information spread to a large number of people in a relatively short period of time. Hence, the chance for rumors and misinformation was significantly decreased. The all-at-once approach reduced the pressure on my family to explain and reexplain the facts as well as deal repeatedly with other people's emotional responses. Concurrently, spouses and family members of other survivors were able to surround my family and tell stories of encouragement and hope.

Our healing community—immediate family (both blood and heart-chosen), friends, medical personnel, and our church—keeps our beings nurtured while our bodies struggle to repair themselves. Beings are not designed to be alone. In saying this, there is, of course, the truth that you are never alone. There is a Being who is with you no matter who else supports and encourages you. That truth can be of tremendous assistance to your body in the process of responding to your health crisis. Remember, as you walk through the valley of the shadow of death, others have walked that valley before. Others have faced death. In fact, if you look carefully as you walk your path, you will see the footprints of God, for even the Being of God took on a human body, knew pain, faced fear, and experienced death, all to demonstrate that more life awaits. In life and in death we belong to God, and I believe that life is what God has in store for my being, and for yours.

1. *Make yourself comfortable, offer this time to God.*
2. *Examine your life and make a list—written or mental—of people for whom you are thankful, particularly those who are a part of your healing.*
3. *Let this Thanksgiving prayer become yours.*
4. *Give thanks to God for what you have experienced in this silent time.*
5. *Conclude with the Lord's Prayer.*

THANKSGIVING FOR PARTNERS IN HEALING

I thank my God for you every time I think of you; and every time I pray for you all, I pray with joy because of the way in which you have helped me in the work of the gospel from the very first day until now. And so I am sure that God, who began this good work in you, will carry it on until it is finished on the Day of Christ Jesus. You are always in my heart! And so it is only right for me to feel as I do about you. For you have all shared with me in this privilege that God has given me. . . .

—PHILIPPIANS 1:3–7

Focus on the faces of the supportive people in your congregation, or
substitute friends, neighbors, coworkers. Remember encouragement you've
received from them. Give thanks for them as you use Divine Reading
(page 29) to reflect on this passage.

THE BLESSING OF COMMUNITY

How wonderful it is, how
pleasant,
for God's people to live together
in harmony!
It is like the precious anointing oil
running down from Aaron's
head and beard,
down to the collar of his robes.
It is like the dew on Mount
Hermon,
falling on the hills of Zion.
That is where the Lord has
promised his blessing—
life that never ends.

—PSALMS 133

Before going on to Chapter 9, use Divine Reading (page 29),
Imaginative Prayer (page 44), or both to explore this passage.

ENCOURAGEMENT

Come to me, all of you who are tired from carrying heavy loads, and I will give you rest. Take my yoke and put it on you, and learn from me, because I am gentle and humble in spirit; and you will find rest.

—MATTHEW 11:28–29

REFLECTIONS

9.

THE SPIRITUAL
SURVIVAL KIT

■

*In our religious striving, we are usually looking for something
quite other than the God who has come looking for us.*

—EUGENE H. PETERSON, *ANSWERING GOD*

As frightening as they are, some diagnoses give us time to plan, to
examine our options, educate ourselves on methods of treatment,
and choose our preferred physicians. Mine did. Bruce's, Sue's, Sally's,
and Sara's did not. Whether your own physical crisis finds you reading this book immediately following diagnosis, in the midst of treatment, or struggling with recovery, know that you do not come to this
time of your life wholly unprepared. You do, in fact, possess at least
the rudimentary elements of a spiritual survival kit.

Living as I do in California, survival kits are an everyday part of
life. Here, they are earthquake survival kits, sold everywhere from
school fund-raisers to sporting goods stores. The kits usually contain

the commonsense basics: candles, matches, batteries, flashlight, and blanket, plus food and water for one or more people, depending on how much you want to pay. Since the question is not if, but when an earthquake will strike, the contents can literally save your life.

The same is true of your spiritual survival kit. The issue is not if a health crisis will occur in an individual, but when, how, and how often. And although the basic elements of your spiritual survival kit may have been provided during your lifetime by parents, pastors, Sunday school teachers, and friends, the kit will serve you best if you build on those early spiritual practices, adding to them and adapting them to fit your own personal relationship with God. Put those elements to work, and the result is a body prepared for healing and open to that which you desire most: the coming of the God who loves you and desires to give you life.

There are four main aspects of a spiritual survival kit. Though I break the categories apart, in reality all overlap, and whether you currently have the "luxury" of examining these elements of survival prior to treatment or are looking at them afterward, developing them now will serve you well. The four categories are spiritual, intellectual, physical, and emotional.

Because of your Christian background, the spiritual aspect of survival is quite probably the area where you have the greatest advance preparation. From the songs we first learn in Sunday school to the prayer and meditation patterns we develop as adults, we have the means of drawing spiritual strength. You are not starting from a vacuum. A straightforward faith is just as effective as complex knowledge of theology, and wherever you are on your spiritual journey, you are already better equipped than you think.

Barbara Patrick calls hers "a simplistic faith." "My prayers are very simple," she says. " 'Thank you for this day and our food and our family.' I ask that I will have the strength and the knowledge to care for my patients." Barbara, a nurse, has had surgery, high-dosage chemotherapy, and a bone marrow transplant for advanced breast cancer. Her deep, unwavering faith has seen her through worse things than breast cancer. though—her youngest daughter, just sixteen years old, died in a boating accident:

"That was far worse than this cancer. It is every parent's nightmare and you never get over it. But I had to keep going. I was single then, and I still had four children. I had to pull myself up and make a living for them. I did what had to be done."

For years, Barbara worked as an oncology nurse and when she discovered a lump in her breast, she knew what lay in store. The discovery itself was surprising, though, as her mammograms had always come back negative. Surgeons found cancer in ten lymph nodes.

"At work people said, 'We knew you were going to come through just fine because of your attitude.' I didn't think I had such a great attitude. But faith and prayer give you the strength to handle the difficult things in life. I read Isaiah and Psalms. I read passages that speak of hardships and make notes by them. I find them comforting in many ways. Still, I don't day by day sit and read my Bible—I get up at 5:30 A.M., shower, eat, throw on some clothes, and get to work."

You can benefit from an intentional increase in your spiritual practices anytime. Immerse yourself in the word. Set aside additional time with God. If necessary, make appointments with yourself to do so, much as you would with doctors. Then take extra time to visit with a pastor or spiritual director. Prepare your spiritual reserves so that when you feel very empty, your faith will be a channel through which God can fill you up.

During the six weeks between my diagnosis and surgery, I requested five additional days of medical leave for spiritual preparation. My treatment had already started and hormone therapy to shrink the tumor had me on an emotional roller coaster, so I was especially grateful to finally get in my car and drive north up the coast. I spent several days at a Christian retreat center working with a spiritual director, and increased my time of Bible study, prayer, and meditation. It was during these days of intense preparation that I had the spiritual experience of Jesus speaking to me in the operating room. Those five days were invaluable time, and in hindsight, had my request for extended medical leave not been granted, I would gladly have given up vacation time or taken an unpaid leave of absence.

When we face any crisis it is helpful to remember the resources God offers. Out of the generosity of divine love, God has made available to us so much more than we could ever hope or desire for ourselves. Using either Divine Reading (page 29) or Imaginative Prayer (page 44), let the words and images of this passage from Isaiah play in your mind. When you come to the promise of "the best food of all," picture what that might be. Do you even know? Listen carefully for the answer.

GOD'S INVITATION TO YOU

The LORD says,
"Come, everyone who is
thirsty—
here is water!
Come, you that have no
money—
buy grain and eat!
Come! Buy wine and milk—
it will cost you nothing!
Why spend money on what does
not satisfy?
Why spend your wages and
still be hungry?
Listen to me and do what I say,
and you will enjoy the best
food of all.

Listen now, my people, and
come to me;
come to me, and you will have
life!"

—ISAIAH 55:1–3

Along with your spiritual resources are intellectual resources, an even easier category to augment, since increasing your knowledge about your disease is nearly unavoidable. Books and articles on prostate cancer began to leap at me from book racks and magazine stands. The Internet fairly shouted information and advice, some very wise, some of little use. Plus, as soon as my cancer was public knowledge, friends both from within and outside the church regularly sent me reading material drawn from all kinds of sources. I am convinced that nothing relating to my disease and its possible treatments slipped unnoticed by those concerned about me. I read many of the publications, and my family and several close friends, who acted as my screening committee, read many more. They highlighted any important points they thought I might want to know and passed the publications on to me.

Overall, I found their efforts extremely helpful. I have talked to other patients, though, who responded quite differently to the wealth of available data. They were simply overwhelmed. In a number of cases they just threw up their hands in defeat, saying. "What can I do with the information anyway?"

There is certainly much that can be done with information. At the time of my diagnosis, I had very little medical knowledge, no experience reading about medical treatment programs, and almost no knowledge about prostate cancer. Like many, I assumed that virtually all men developed prostate cancer at some time in their lives and that, if caught early, prostate cancer was 100 percent curable. Only through reading and talking with doctors did I discover that there were many manifestations of prostate cancer, some much more curable than others. I was not pleased to learn that prostate cancer is the second largest killer of men in the United States, second only to heart disease.

Yet through my research, I determined early on that I had responsibility for my own treatment program. The doctors and medical people were trained specialists available to assist me in the process of healing—a process that God had already designed into my body and being. I asked so many questions that one doctor described me in his medical report as "an overly anxious patient with a more-than-average knowledge of the disease"—I know, because en route to yet another examining room, charts in hand, I read through my own medical records. I must say, I take the physician's comment as a compliment. Dr. Siegel has observed in his surgical practice that survivors of illness "are rarely docile. They retain control of their lives. They are intelligent, with a strong sense of reality."[1] I see nothing insulting there.

The educational process did enable me to take charge of the healing of my body. Created in the image of God, I did have the freedom to choose what happened to me. I set about gathering as much information as possible and eventually came to trust my own ability to discern what was happening in my body and to make appropriate decisions in response. Intellectual resources enabled me to be more actively involved in my treatment than I otherwise would have been, and that involvement in itself was wonderfully healing.

[1] Bernie S. Siegel, M.D., *Love, Medicine & Miracles.* Harper & Row, New York, 1986.

What information do you need to better make decisions about your course of action? What resources are available to you? What decisions concerning your treatment or course of action are still ahead of you? Repeated meditation on the same verse can help focus our thinking and our plans of action. Use Divine Reading (page 29) to meditate on these words.

MEDITATION ON TRUTH

You will know the truth, and the truth shall set you free.

—JOHN 8:32

An important aspect of intellectual survival skills is talking with patients as well as doctors other than your own. Since you are free to take responsibility for your own treatment, you are free to consult as many doctors as you wish concerning your diagnosis and ongoing treatment program. Good doctors not only welcome but encourage other opinions. Physicians know that their work is as much art as science (it is called the "practice" of medicine for a reason). Your doctor and hospital will make available to you on request your records and other pertinent information. I ultimately talked with five urologists before choosing both my doctor and the treatment program he recommended.

I may have been an overly anxious patient. I may have asked more questions than normal and even irritated the doctors at times. I entered treatment, however, with much greater confidence in the program I had chosen. The confidence that comes from mentally strengthening yourself to make informed decisions about your own treatment is an important ingredient in the healing process.

Physical conditioning is the third element of your survival kit. Its purpose is to offer the body that God has given you the maximum opportunity for health. For me, this physical aspect took multiple forms—the first, more than usual amounts of rest. I had to give myself permission to take naps several times each day, even if they were only a few minutes long. I also had to give myself permission to leave evening meetings early or to cut short social times in order to be in bed at a decent time. Neither of these behaviors had been part of my normal mode of operation, and I was only able to successfully maintain this pattern when I saw rest as an important part of the treatment of my disease.

Prior to surgery, I augmented regular walks with special exercises to prepare the part of the body that would be most intensely affected. I also added a regimen of daily sit-ups to help strengthen the site of the pending incision. My physical exercise continues to this day, supported by an increasingly health-conscious diet—I've been amazed to find how important diet is to our overall health. The staff at the blood bank steered me initially toward certain high-iron foods, and since then I've solicited the help of nutritionists and delved into specialized diets. You will find your own approach to this element of your survival kit. If it is longer life you desire, the important point is to work both with your physicians and with the Great Physician to assist your body.

The final resource is emotional strength, an area, of course, closely connected to all other aspects of survival. A friend of mine, Lee Schmidt, is an expert in this area. Early in her career as a registered nurse, Lee struggled to cope with the professional hazards of grief and depression that came particularly when working with children's catastrophic illnesses. When Lee suggested to the head of the Ohio State Nurses Association that a program for handling emotional onslaught be developed, the idea was turned down, flat. "She said no one would be interested," Lee remembers. Later, Lee relocated to a job at the University of California at Los Angeles and entered pediatric oncology. At that point, she took matters into her own hands:

"I worked closely with one particular family for a long time. They had a little girl named Sandy, who was diagnosed at age three with cancer. They fought it hard and she had years of remission, but the cancer came back when she was thirteen. I saw how much that family loved her. I went to the funeral.

"By then I was teaching and I was able to start a support group for the nurses. The nurses would talk about families they were concerned about, families for which they weren't able to identify any existing support system—friends, family ties. When a child is in the hospital, you have all the support of the doctors and nurses, the counselors at the hospital. But once you leave the hospital, that's the end of your support ties."

At the nudging of the nurses Lee launched a similar support program for parents. Soon she was inundated with pleas for help.

Lee counseled for twelve years, and in that time personally dealt with some five hundred people, helping them recognize the need to articulate their feelings and draw strength from sharing.

"I felt especially sorry for the men, because they couldn't express their pain as easily as women. There was this one man who would get into his car, drive around, and scream. He would scream all the way to work—the only safe place to express himself was going sixty miles per hour on the freeway. Since then, on the freeway, I've seen other people screaming by themselves. I don't know why their pain is there, but I can see it.

"How much God works through people—in the support group, they reach out to comfort each other. They give each other permission to cry and to laugh, and by doing so, they're giving each other permission to live.

"Ill children support each other instinctively. I remember one little kid who had to have a brain tumor removed—the bandages made the head look like a balloon. This bandaged child was in its bed when another sick child was brought in and put in the next bed over. The new child was sobbing and sobbing, 'I want my mother!' The first little kid watched, eyes wide open, then reached through the bars of the bed and said, 'I'll be your mother.' "

During this time, Lee found herself in desperate need of emotional strength, losing two children, one at birth and one through miscarriage, and in her quest for healing, came to appreciate how closely emotional strength and spiritual strength are tied:

"I saw in my counseling how much faith helped in regaining emotional strength, and I felt sorry for the people who didn't have any faith to fall back on. At the very least we have God to get angry at, instead of the people we love. We have someone we can point a finger at, and that helps. God can take all the anger we have. If God is God, he can handle that and more.

"When my first child, Matthew, died, it was like I had been betrayed. I had prayed to God for a healthy child and I felt a promise had been broken. I felt absolutely abandoned. That was the time I walked away from my faith.

"There were two things that helped.

"I have a friend, a very unique lady who is an absolute agnostic. She has had an awful life in many ways, some her own doing. But she has always been envious of my faith, of the comfort I find in it, and wishes she had it. She was so upset when I lost the baby and pulled away from my faith that she tried desperately to find me a Christian counselor. I don't remember if she didn't find one, or if she did and I didn't go, but the fact that she tried so hard was very important to me.

"And then I came across a book, written by a pastor whose son had been killed in a car accident two blocks from home. It was the story of a man of faith who had grappled with his faith. The conclusion that he came to was one I now absolutely believe: God has an overwhelming love for us. The only thing we can possibly compare to it is being a parent. When your child simply falls down and scrapes its knee, as a parent, you die a little. God is somebody who cries before I even cry. He doesn't bring hurt to our lives, but cries for us when hurt comes."

Lee and her husband went on to adopt two children, and delighted in their family of four. Then Lee was diagnosed with breast cancer. Between her supportive friends, her clinical experience, and her faith, she was emotionally steady. "I had no doubts about surgery," she says. "Faced with life or breast, I'll take life every time."

Emotional strength is obviously a crucial component of survival. By allowing her emotions to be nurtured by friends, Lee had the maximum positive emotional energy to focus on her body. You may already have your own favorite means of emotionally pampering yourself. For myself, I found pre- and post-surgery important times to be with the friends I cared deeply about. Some friends I was able to visit physically, some only by phone. The laughter and shared joy, the conversation and shared tears were a real tonic to my soul. I also found it nurturing to spend time in activities I loved, in places I loved: a drive along the coast, a walk on the beach, a trip to the mountains, activities centered wherever I had felt the presence of God and the fullness of life in the past.

Developing the tools for confronting a health crisis takes a deliberate effort and an acknowledgment that you are important enough to set aside time and energy for healing. The effort pays off. The benefits that intentional meditation can bring to us as people of faith are both a gift from God and a pathway by which God comes to us.

Use Divine Reading (page 29), Imaginative Prayer (page 44), or both. Remember that for a person of faith, even the death of the body is not defeat.

AFFIRMATION OF TRUST IN GOD

I come to you, LORD, for protection;
never let me be defeated.
You are a righteous God;
save me, I pray!
Hear me! Save me now!
Be my refuge to protect me;
my defense to save me.

You are my refuge and defense;
guide me and lead me as you
have promised.
Keep me safe from the trap that
has been set for me;
shelter me from danger.
I place myself in your care.
You will save me, LORD;
you are a faithful God.

—PSALMS 31:1—5

10.

HOLY PLACES,
HEALING PLACES

Who is this coming from the
desert,
arm in arm with her lover?

—SONG OF SONGS 8:5

Imagine you've been separated from the love of your life, and now the time is coming when you will be reunited. You can hardly wait. You clean your house so it looks wonderful and smells even better. You set out flowers and light the candles. You cook your beloved's favorite foods. You get a surprise gift and a special card and carefully select the music. And from the preparation, from its anticipation, comes a heightened sensory awareness. The joy in the reunion is immense.

It is possible to prepare for the God who comes to us. While our preparations don't make God come any more than they make our beloved come, by the mere act of our preparation we make ourselves more open to the presence of God. By carefully preparing the setting, we can create our own places of heightened awareness, our own "holy" places.

Already there are places in our world where people seem to consistently be more aware of God's presence. The early Israelites identified Mt. Sinai and the Temple in Jerusalem as places where they perceived God to be especially active. They also had a sacred, portable Tent of the Lord's Presence, which provided a constantly visible, tangible location where they were acutely aware of the coming of God.

Christians, likewise, have their holy places. Some are great churches and cathedrals, such as St. Peter's in Rome, St. Paul's in London, and Notre Dame in Paris; some are shrines as in Lourdes, France, or Fatima, Portugal. Some holy places are simply geographic: just off the western coast of Scotland is a beautiful little island called Iona, where Colomba of Iona introduced Christianity to the Scots in the sixth century. A monastery or convent has existed there since that time and it was there that Scottish Presbyterian George MacLeod founded the Christian Iona Community, describing Iona as a thin place in the universe where the sacred and the secular meet.

Individually, we have those places where for us God is more active, more present. It may be a home church where we grew up or a Christian camp. It may be some outdoor setting: the beach, the mountains, a lakeside cabin where we go when we want to feel particularly close to God. Prior to surgery I went for several days to a retreat house in Los Altos, California, the place where I had been introduced to the Ignatian exercises. It was a full day's drive from my home, yet I did not go there because I thought that God was more present there. I went because in that place I quickly and easily open to the God who faithfully seeks to come to me, and yet seems to have difficulty getting my attention in other places.

Little introspection is necessary to realize that the God who comes to us, the God who is the creator of the whole world, "does not live in temples made by human hands" (Acts 17:24). God is not confined to any space, be it a building or shrine which we as human beings have made, or a place of natural beauty. God is not more present in a church building or a conference ground than in the heart of the city or the most remote areas of our planet. God is God and comes and goes at divine will, not ours. We cannot build a building or choose a setting beautiful enough to make God come to us. On Sunday when we gather with other Christians to worship, we do not go to a spot where God is more present than where we daily work and play. Rather, we go where we are more open, more focused on God, more aware of the every-moment reality of the divine presence. God is not more in one place than in another. I am more aware of the presence of God in some places than in others.

The good news is that there are things we can do to allow places to become for us more holy. We can transform any ordinary space into a place where we are more naturally aware of the God who is already present.

Lee Kliewer is eighty-three years old, the next to the youngest of fifteen children born to a German farming Mennonite pastor's family. An ordained Presbyterian minister, Lee served as a chaplain in the armed forces during World War II, pastor of several churches, and Stated Clerk of the Synod of Southern California and Hawaii. After his "retirement" at age seventy, he served as interim pastor at several churches before hearing loss caused him to truly retire at age eighty. I have known Lee for more than a decade as a member of a monthly support group of five pastors who meet to comfort and confront, encourage and support one another.

During those years I have learned by bits and pieces the recent crises Lee has endured. He seldom talks about any of his problems and I have never heard him name them all at one time. Lee's prostate cancer was discovered only after the tumor had spread beyond the prostate, and radiation has produced lingering side effects. His continual and increasing loss of hearing has forced him even to resign from volunteer boards of agencies he loves. Acute eye trouble, uncertain balance, and prostate problems requiring surgery are ongoing. In spite of his physical limitations he has created for himself, on the side of a hill, his own, private, holy place where he celebrates life and God through prayer:

"There's been a peace and comfort in my life that has almost nothing to do with what's going on either inside my body or outside. This is the richest time of my life—I have never had it so good. I appreciate everything God has made far more than I did when I was busy. Every morning and every evening, the sunrise and the sunset are so meaningful. There's a hill God has given us behind our house, where I've created a two- or three-mile trail. I climb that trail every other day, at least. I have my 'prayer chairs' which are increasingly also my resting chairs. God floods his love into my life. I am thankful for my life, whatever it might be."

Holy places are yours to create, and the transformation from ordinary area to extraordinary space is certainly possible with a hospital room and with any location where you will spend time healing.

The first step in transforming space is to prepare your mind. For scheduled hospital stays, you might request permission, as I did, to spend some time in silence in your soon-to-be hospital room. In silence I invited God to be present with me, hoping my invitation would make me aware of God's continual presence. I thought about what would happen in the room, pictured the experiences in as much detail as possible, and offered all my thoughts to God.

The second step is to prepare the room visually, much as we do when we prepare a sanctuary for worship. For my room, I gathered together a Bible, several other books, and some vases—fresh flowers to me are a symbol of beauty and joy and a reminder of the extravagant generosity of God. To either side of my bed I had pictures of family, positioned so that when the people I loved arrived, they would remember how important they were to me and know how much I counted on them to be a part of the healing I so desired.

I placed two other snapshots on a table at the foot of my bed where I could easily see them, even through the drug-hazed vision of recovery. The photos were of myself on two of my favorite adventures. In one, I was with a small group of friends at the top of the highest ski run at Mammoth Lakes. It was a beautifully sunny day and we were in full ski gear ready to make the run down the mountain. The other picture was from a river raft trip down the Kern River. Another man from our church and I were in a two-seated "splash yak" coming through some wild rapids. Raging waters allowed only our helmeted heads and part of the intense blue of the boat to peek through the white froth.

Both of these photographs I placed by my hospital bed represented times of exuberant joy and warm friendships, and made me smile. The pictures were symbols of encouragement and called me to health, inviting me to do whatever was necessary to have a body able to experience those times again. With my Bible, my books, flowers, and my photos in place, visually the hospital room I might have feared was now filled with memories and inspiration and hope.

Pause now and remember times, places, and people that let you feel most healthy and alive, and give thanks.

THANKSGIVING FOR WHOLENESS

+ Offer this time of prayer to God.
+ Ask God for the grace to remember experiences when you were physically healthy.
+ Think back to times you felt most healthy, most alive.
+ Picture the setting.
+ Picture the people who were present.
+ Remember the feelings you had.
+ Remember what it was that enabled you to feel alive.
+ See all of the experiences you have pictured as gifts from God.
+ Give thanks to God for your faith and for all God has given to you.
+ Say the Lord's Prayer.

The third step is to focus on the sounds in a healing room, which are as important as the visual aspects. For me, music was vital. During the week prior to surgery I listened to some of my favorite Christian tapes, and three days before the operation I found myself awake in the middle of the night. It was a pleasant and joyous awakening—in contrast to the frustrating type of awakenings when I have had too much caffeine too late in the evening—and what made this interruption nice was that a treasured praise song was going through my head. I slipped back into sleep. Later I awoke to a different praise song. Throughout the next four hours I woke up repeatedly, always with a different song faintly floating through my mind. I arose about six in the morning, interestingly enough more rested than after a full night's sleep. The experience continued—a variety of songs played in my head throughout that day, that night again, and into the following day. During the second day I finally acknowledged that this was not just a matter of songs stuck in my head. The music became for me a gift of reassurance from God in the immediate hours prior to surgery.

Music is a powerful channel to communicate our faith. Select your favorite tapes of inspirational music to take with you to treatment or surgery. They will lift your spirit much as great music does in the context of worship. I focused on two tapes: One was a selection of contemporary and classical songs of faith performed on piano and flute. The other tape was a collection of old hymns, freshly arranged for piano and voice by our minister of music, Jack Walker. Your own selections, of course, will reflect your taste. Whatever music you choose, it will help make your space a sacred place where you can be more open to the coming of the Great Physician.

The fourth step is the sense of smell. In creating your holy space, it would be a mistake to ignore the importance of scent. A sickroom smell will hardly enhance the healing process. Much can be done to change the scent of a room, provided any roommates don't object. Potpourri, mild room scents, even decent mouthwash can remind us of the fragrance of God's love, and open us to that God who desires to come.

As I prepared to transform my hospital space and then my rooms at home into places that affirmed my desire to welcome God I found it helpful to make a list:

+ Bible
+ Pictures of hope and healing
+ Tape recorder, earphones, and meditation tapes
+ Journal/notepad
+ Inspirational books
+ Inspirational videotapes
+ Phone numbers of close friends

Not listed and truly vital are the people you love. Immediate family, both blood and heart-chosen, are valuable parts of the healing community that keep our beings nurtured while our bodies repair themselves. Visits from my family in those first days after surgery were more important to my healing than I can describe. The touches and joy my loved ones brought were soothing medication to me and the visits were good medicine for them as well, even though, as far as looks were concerned, I was in no condition to receive visitors. The comments from my daughters traced both their anxiety and their relief. My daughter Elizabeth remembers my horrible appearance and my less than coherent conversation: "You would talk to us, but then you'd doze, then talk, then doze, then talk. You'd go in and out . . ."

More than longing for communication, my daughter Sarah was looking specifically for an end to the worry that had lived in our home for what seemed like ages: "It was almost a relief to see you in the hospital, because by then the tumor was out of your body and you were already beginning to heal. Physically, you felt worse. Mentally, it seemed like you felt much, much better." My family ended up as guardians of my holy space, limiting visitors, screening phone calls, and making sure I put primary energy into healing.

No one knows better about creating holy space than Marvin Davis, a Christian who lives in an oceanside community just south of me. Marvin has been through two bouts of non-Hodgkin's lymphoma, triple bypass surgery, and now has harnessed prayer to create a healing environment as he adjusts to life as a paraplegic.

The non-Hodgkin's lymphoma came first, appearing initially two decades ago. At that point Marvin made a clear decision not to let the cancer become the focal point of his life. "It was going to be an inconvenience, it would cause me to alter my lifestyle in some respects, but it was something that I was going to overcome," he remembers.

The greater change, though, was on the horizon. In 1998, Marvin and his wife had had a remarkable summer—a fiftieth wedding anniversary celebration in Hawaii with all five grown children, spouses, and a flock of grandchildren, followed by a trip to Denver, Colorado, to visit friends. Marvin wrote off chest pains as a side effect of Denver's high altitude, but on returning home he contacted his doctor. Tests showed a previous angioplasty had failed and that heart surgery was required. When he awakened after a triple bypass procedure, he discovered he could not move his legs.

"I went from being a fairly healthy person to, I didn't know exactly what . . . just overnight," Marvin says. Doctors argued over the cause, but the fact remained that their patient was immobilized from the waist down. Marvin reached for his old cancer-survival philosophy and modified it to fit—paralysis was not going to be the most important thing in his life. And starting that first day, he created a litany of praise and repeated it over and over, out loud: "Praise God I am alive. Praise God I have my mind. I can think. I can make decisions, I can be a normal human being in most respects, except that I can't use my legs." Marvin then listed all the things he was thankful for: his wife and their fifty years together, his children, grandchildren, pastors, neighbors, and friends. "I did wonder what people would think if they walked in and heard me talking to my God," he says.

The litany traveled with him from the surgical ward to the rehabilitation hospital and he leaned on it as he received more bad news. "After a few days it dawned on me that all we were working on was how to maneuver in a wheelchair. So I asked the counselor when we were going to work on my legs. It was his unfortunate task to tell me that I was not going to be able to walk again, ever."

As unlikely as it seems, that moment spawned a lasting friendship. The spiritual strength that Marvin drew from his litany helped him embark on a discussion of faith with the counselor, who turned out to be a Christian himself. Their subsequent frank conversations, as one Christian to another, gave a different air to the rehab efforts. With help, Marvin built up the muscles in his upper body, figured out how to dress himself and how to manage life in general. "I learned all the marvelous things they can teach you to do when you cannot use your legs at all," he says.

When the time came to reconcile himself to his new life at home, Marvin brought his positive attitude and prayer litany with him. The holy, healing space that prayer generated at the rehabilitation center is now portable.

"I continued that prayer for a long, long time. I still use it, not aloud as in the early days, but I think it. It is the thing I hold on to. I can almost feel it in my hand, the love of God, the greatest power in creation, that will never, never, never let me go."

When you create your own holy place, you remind yourself that God has come to you in the past and will again. Your creation will not dictate God's arrival, but it will enhance the moments of uniting when the coming occurs. And if the coming does not occur on your schedule, all is not lost. You will still have the benefit of the beauty, the sounds, the scents you have added to your environment. You can still trust that God desires to be with you, and you can look forward to the lover of your soul arriving on another occasion soon.

For God is the divine lover of us all, clearly demonstrating in Jesus Christ a devoted interest in our health and well-being. We can wait with open arms physically, spiritually, mentally, and emotionally. We can arrange our space to welcome healing. And we can do it all with confidence, because God has made clear that there is nothing that he will not do to make us whole.

Spend some time with Psalm 84. Use Divine Reading (page 29),
Imaginative Prayer (page 44), or both as you examine your own
response to your awareness of the presence of God.

RESPONSE TO THE AWARENESS OF GOD

How I love your Temple,
Lord Almighty!
How I want to be there!
I long to be in the Lord's
Temple.
With my whole being I sing for joy
to the living God.
Even the sparrows have built a
nest,
and the swallows have their own
home;
they keep their young near your
altars,
Lord Almighty, my king and
my God.
How happy are those who live in
your Temple,
always singing praise to you. . . .

One day spent in your Temple
is better than a thousand
anywhere else;
I would rather stand at the gate of
the house of my God

than live in the homes of the
wicked.
The LORD is our protector and
glorious king,
blessing us with kindness and honor.
He does not refuse any good
thing
to those who do what is right.
LORD Almighty, how happy are
those who trust in you!

—PSALMS 84:1–4, 10–12

. . . .

. . . .

. . . .

. . . .

. . . .

. . . .

. . . .

. . . .

. . . .

. . . .

. . . .

. . . .

. . . .

. . . .

. . . .

. . . .

. . . .

. . . .

. . . .

Before going on to Chapter 11, use the patterns of Divine Reading (page 29), Imaginative Prayer (page 44), or both to explore Psalm 112.

CAUSE FOR CONFIDENCE

Happy is the person who honors
the LORD,
who takes pleasure in obeying
his commands. . . .

He is not afraid of receiving bad
news;
his faith is strong, and he trusts
in the LORD.
He is not worried or afraid;
he is certain to see his enemies
defeated.

—PSALMS 112:1, 7–8

11.

THE GIFT OF
GRATITUDE

I love the LORD, because
he hears me;
he listens to my prayers.
He listens to me
every time I call to him. . . .
he stopped my tears
and kept me from defeat.
And so I walk in the presence of
the LORD
in the world of the living.

—PSALMS 116:1–2, 8–9

It has now been several years since I discovered that my body contained cancer. I have completed surgery and several forms of radiation treatment, and I am stumbling along, trying to get my body to function as it did before. I have not had full recovery and doctors indicate I may never be quite the same physically. I know I will never be the same spiritually.

What has been the result of this journey? Deepened friendships, certainly. New friends. A great appreciation of what others have experienced in illness, an intense awareness of the finite nature of life, a reinforcement of the value of love relationships—and those results are just a fraction of what I could name. There is another plus, one that overarches the rest: the infusion of gratitude into my life. I have always tended to be a grateful person, appreciating whatever I had or did, but the experience of being face-to-face with a deadly illness took what gratitude I had worked with and propelled it to new heights. I find myself walking around constantly saying "thank you," sometimes to other people, sometimes to myself, always to God.

The first time I ventured out to public worship was four weeks after surgery. I was physically quite capable—the surgery had gone better than I had been led to anticipate. My family and I went to visit some friends in another community and it was a delight to have the rare opportunity to sit with my wife and daughters in a worship service. I did well emotionally until the first hymn, a favorite of mine for years: "Praise ye the Lord, the Almighty, the King of creation! O my soul, praise him, for he is thy health and salvation." I was able to sing that far and then I started to cry, throwing my teenage daughters into an awkward mixture of concern and acute embarrassment. What they did not know and what in the context of worship I could not tell them, was that far from tears of pain or sadness, these were tears of gratitude for the One who had designed me, the One who now literally had become my source of wholeness—my "health and salvation." Ignatius called such tears a consolation, when emotion is unexpectedly aroused and the soul is inflamed with love of its Creator. The opposite had been desolation, the place where I had started: physically restless, emotionally in turmoil, and closed down to divine love in my life. In that moment of worship, I was consoled.

Today it is still almost impossible for me to make it through communion without crying. Remembering the words of Christ, "This is my body, *broken for you*," unleashes in me feelings that are new, powerful, and profound. During a return visit to a Christian retreat center, five months after surgery and two days after completing radiation therapy, I went into the chapel. There is one line in the preparation for the Eucharist that I had heard dozens of times before, but never in the way I heard it that morning: "Lamb of God who takes away the sins of the world, *only say the word and I will be healed.*" In that moment, that prayer embodied the hope I needed. To the God who comes, I could only echo the psalmist's words, and say, "Thank you."

Today I watch in awe the lives of those whose crises are even more dire than mine—and whose thankfulness is more intense. Lee Kliewer's string of health ailments was more than enough to leave most people disappointed at best, and more likely, embittered and angry. Instead, Lee, who died during the writing of this manuscript, was one of the most joyful, grateful human beings I have ever met. That remained true until the end of his life. Lee knew that life is a gift, and though I have always said I believed that as well, the philosophy is now central to my faith. Each relationship, each new thought, each event is a marvelous flavor bud with value and meaning, exploding forth like popcorn out of a tiny kernel.

A gift does not just appear on its own, of course, it necessitates a giver. So it is with the gift of life. Whether the joys of life come to us through the work of our own hands or through the actions of other people, they are a gift from God. God's history holds a clear pattern of giving. God gave the created order to all creatures, including human beings, as a free gift. God gave Joseph dreams, the Israelites freedom, and Moses the Law. God gave life to Daniel and the message to the prophets. God gave confidence to Elizabeth and

Mary. Ultimately, the intensity of God's love gave us forgiveness and grace through Jesus Christ, the greatest gift of all.

What is it about the nature of God that causes God to give? Could it be that God practices what Jesus preached, "It is more of a blessing to give than to receive"? Could it be that God not only loves "a cheerful giver" (the Greek word is *hilaros*, God loves a "hilarious giver"), but that God, too, has a hilarious time giving?[1] Could it be that God's generosity creates divine joy just as our giving creates joy for us?

Whatever the answer, the pattern is clear. Life is a gift. A gift necessitates a giver, and as people of faith, we know that giver to be God. It only makes sense, in our times of greatest need, that God continues to come, giving life.

So Lee Kliewer continued to hike to his prayer chairs, celebrating God's love flooding into his life, and despite the progression of age-related illness, gave thanks until the end.

And what about the others, the people whose stories we have shared?

The happy toddler on Sally Anderson's lap is a testament to the power of Sally's faith and to her strength of will. Christopher, the youngest of the Anderson family's six children, is now well launched into childhood. With help, he has overcome his initial neurological damage and romps and learns right alongside his brothers and sisters. Sally herself still struggles with the aftereffects of her stroke—she battles fatigue, and late at night, speech difficulties. On the other hand, she is also enrolled in the local college and is currently taking calculus, on her way to obtaining her bachelor's degree in mathematics.

From Jim Huffstutler's viewpoint, he's very healthy: "I'm hardly ever sick. I just get the big stuff—brain tumors, broken legs, hearts that stop." Those big things have taken their toll. His wife broke down under the strain, leaving Jim to raise their two children alone,

[1] 2 Corinthians 9:7.

and the limits to his mobility are such that the hospital got him a handicap placard. Still, his absolute trust is that God is unfailingly with him. "My faith is almost one that I'm ashamed to say I just take advantage of," he says.

Beyond warranting him a good parking place, the handicaps don't reach Jim's consciousness:

"A brain surgeon in a hospital elevator once pointed at me and said, 'What's wrong with you?' I said, 'Nothing. What's wrong with you?' Maybe I'm a person of denial . . . or maybe it's a matter of living with what you have and not despairing over what you don't have. There's a scene in the film *Monty Python and the Holy Grail* where a knight is guarding a bridge. His adversary has a sword and keeps slicing off parts of the knight's body. Off go his arms, off go his legs, but the defiant knight keeps saying, 'It's just a flesh wound' and 'I've had worse.' Finally, it's just his torso bouncing around, yelling.

"For me, okay so my brain goes, so my heart goes, so my vision goes, but you'll never stop me. As long as we have a day, it's a gift."

Howard Rice has spent the last thirty years smoking like a madman, hoping lung cancer might kill him before his multiple sclerosis spread above his waist and at last took over his body completely. Peculiarly, the paralysis never spread and now we know why. Just months ago, Howard was handed a totally new diagnosis: transverse myelitis—a spinal cord severed by infection. He never had MS at all. First, when he got the news, he cried from utter relief. Then he quit smoking.

Howard is currently coupling Western medicine with all kinds of alternative approaches on a new crusade for health. He is exploring acupuncture, magnets, hypnotherapy, vitamin and mineral supplements, and therapy/support groups. "There's not much I won't try, as long as it's clearly not going to hurt me," he says. Still in a wheelchair, he works out in a gym, swims in a pool, and has shed thirty pounds. He is trying to cooperate with his body's own healing powers, just in case his nerve cells are trying to regenerate.

"I can't say it has made a huge difference so far," Howard says. "I can feel a little more sensation in my right leg, I'm able to straighten my knees out in bed, and by the end of the day, my feet hurt, which is odd. It may not be enough to make me stand up and walk before I leave this planet, but something is happening."

Around his neck he wears a crucifix, to remind him of the one who is with us in our suffering. "That's the image of Christ I find most important," he says. "Not Jesus the Fixer, but Jesus the one who suffers with us." And he has become a survivor: "Not a survivor from death, but a survivor from despair, a survivor from being controlled by a disease."

Marvin Davis still refuses to let illness or its aftermath hold him back. He has served communion twice since he has been paralyzed. The latest occasion was on Ash Wednesday, with his daughter. He also recently got word that he is officially cured of cancer. "I think God wants me to do something," he says. "I want to be helpful to other people as I have been helped. I have had the privilege of living in this great creation and wonderful things continue to happen to me. There's a feeling that is different from any I've ever, ever had, when I wake up, look out my window, and see it's another beautiful day."

While Sara Jackson's treatments for Crohn's disease continue, off and on, she can also be seen running the hills of Southern California with her Dalmatian. Sara values life, certainly enough to wince as she hands the car keys to her son, now sixteen years old and the holder of a brand-new driver's license. She has left freeway driving instruction to her husband. Of her illness, she says, "It changed our lives, it changed the way we see things. It brought our family closer than we ever were before."

Barbara Patrick has returned to her nursing career. Her hair, the first thing to go with chemotherapy, has now grown back to about two inches in length and she just goes to work with it that way. "It's too hot to wear a wig," she says. Barbara puts her own chances for a complete cure at 75 percent. She swims a couple of times a week, gives thanks for the help of her husband, and instead of praying for herself, she prays for other friends who are ill. "Enough prayer time has been spent on me."

With three major surgeries behind her, Connie Wintler focuses on the strength that prayer partners provide. "Because I didn't tell anyone about my first surgery it took me ten years to mourn the loss of my breast. Now I'm in a support group. They help you walk through emotional pain and it's cleansing. I do miss my breasts, but you adapt. There's really no alternative."

It might surprise you to know that, throughout a successful career committed to helping others through emotional pain, Lee Schmidt herself has always lived with constant physical pain. She was born without hip sockets and her memories of childhood are laced with visions of surgical suites and a six-month stay at Shriner's Hospital. She has limped all of her life. Yet her self-image is so strong it simply overwhelms both her lifelong physical limitations and her recent round with breast cancer. Lee does not think of herself as a cancer survivor. When I introduced her to someone, and said, "She's a cancer survivor, too," Lee was shocked. "That's not a label I put on myself," she says. "I'm still surprised when I look in a shop window and see myself limping. I don't even think of myself as a person who limps." And her response to life is one of gratitude.

"Right after my surgery, I wrote a generic 'thank-you' letter," Lee says. "I started out, 'Many good things have happened since I was diagnosed with breast cancer two months ago.' Then I listed all the wonderful things people had done. They stopped their lives for a moment to make a meal, to buy a card. They made a conscious decision to help. Thanking them was good for me, too. It made me remember how people reach out."

Friends' attempts at reaching out to the Kunz family after Sue's chiropractic accident were at first more frustrating than helpful. "All those people in the hospital waiting room would say, 'If there's anything I can do to help, just call.' It got to be irritating," John says. "Yes, I needed help, but they never really offered anything concrete and I didn't even know what to ask."

Then one day, he discovered the gift God had been giving all along:

"A young couple said the usual 'What can we do to help?' I turned around and said, 'I don't know. What can you do?' My question caught them by surprise. Then the woman, Nancy, said, 'I'm just a beautician.'

"Just a beautician? Sue had been horizontal for over a month and we had to figure out how to get her into a wheelchair, but from that day on, Nancy would do her hair. It was such a little thing for Nancy and such a big hurdle for me. Afterward, when people said, 'If there's anything I can do . . . ,' I automatically asked, 'What are you willing to do?' Then they began to get specific: 'We have a spare bedroom'; 'We can baby-sit.' That was information I could use.

"About this same time, I went to visit a pastor who had been hospitalized due to an accident. After a while I ran out of things to talk about and I said, 'Well, if there's anything I can do . . .'

"I stopped there and started to laugh. I said, 'Let me rephrase. If you need some pastoral duties done, people called on, people prayed for, you give me their names and I'll do that for you.'

"Now I am a totally different pastor. We lived five and a half months in a hospital, and I came out knowing more about people's pain. It might be because of an accident or a wayward child or cancer, but everyone has a hurting heart. Today I can minister to their pain. If you pay attention to how God works with you, you can be a minister to others.

"I still have days when I go to my office and say, 'God, I am really angry at you. I hate watching Sue struggle and you haven't changed things. Sometimes I talk to God for one minute, sometimes for a half hour, and I always end up in praise and worship because he's big enough to handle all that I feel.

"I'm going to keep walking on. We can crumple in a pile and cry or we can get up, keep going, and see what God will do. I visualize God is looking at me, nodding his head 'yes,' grinning and saying, 'It's okay, hold on to that. Keep walking.'"

Walking is exactly what Bruce Gossard does, today literally. Medical science and his faith have served him well. Married, with a daughter and a son, he is no longer the bitter young man who questioned any promises God made.

Early in his crisis, Bruce had written: "Did I deserve this wretched fate? If there is a god, he's a god of hate!" Concluding his letter to me in my time of trouble, he revealed God's healing:

A year after losing my right leg, I lay in bed sick at heart and hopeless in the early hours of a Sunday morning. I had lost interest in changing channels and accidentally had left the TV tuned to an evangelical program. When the preacher promised that Jesus would heal me right then and there, I was so desperate that I took a step of faith. With him, I raised my arms and hands upward and asked, "Jesus, please come into my life as you have promised you would. Thank you, Lord, for healing me."

These were simple words. Yet I was shaken to the core of my heart and mind when, real as the air I was breathing, the Holy Spirit stepped into my life at once and unmistakably. I couldn't really explain what had happened, I just knew something big had changed.

A couple of days later, I wandered into a local Presbyterian church and met the youth minister. I shared my experience with him as best I could. He helped me get started with Bible study and to get restarted with school and the world.

It's twenty-five years later, now. Did I find truth? Did life become the easy pathway I was looking for? Well . . . yes and no, sort of, but different. I was mistaken about many things, but I did find a really Good Friend to share my troubles and joys with.

One who always understands and never judges. You know him well. I've seen you with him.

Bruce's letter concluded with this poem:

THANKS TO A FRIEND
(THOUGHTS AT AGE 44)

Thank you, Lord, you stand, unmoving.
While I curse, you're waiting, loving.
You take my hand, I cannot speak.
I bow my head; tears come; I'm weak.

Where I saw what life lacked for me,
You saw what good would come to be.
When I was hopeless, wished to die,
You gave me life and reasons why.

Dear Lord, you died in agony
So I might live life endlessly.
In your kingdom, grant me to stand
Beside you, Lord, at your command.

—BRUCE GOSSARD

God is not just a giver, but a lavish one. God creates rain for the just and the unjust. God creates flowers, trees, and a host of natural wonders no one ever sees. God in Christ, with generous abandonment, turned gallons of water into the finest of wine, fed five thousand people with baskets of food to spare, and provided fish so abundant the catch almost sank the disciples' boat. Jesus' stories are filled with the bountiful generosity of God: The prodigal's father pulls out all the stops for his son's return party. Total strangers are invited to the banquet of God, and one-hour workers are paid a full day's wages.

I have gone back repeatedly to the 23rd Psalm. I can now inhale the fragrance of that great Psalm, each phrase bursting open with nourishment for my soul. In a recent meditation, I was drawn to the phrase "You prepare a banquet for me, where all my enemies can see me . . ." A banquet. Not a snack, not a lunch, not a light supper, not an early-bird special. A *banquet*. An extravagant feast.

As I continued to quite literally savor the phrase, an image came to my mind. It was a picture of a great table, perhaps in some medieval castle. The table was spread with an amazing array of food. There were meats and vegetables, cheeses and pastas, breads and pastries, fruits and desserts, beautiful decanters of wine, candles flickering, and a fire dancing in a great fireplace. I was seated at the head of the table as the guest of honor, with servers intent on my every wish. At the far end of the table there were eyes—beady, hungry eyes—watching and desiring what I had. They were the eyes of the cancer cells watching as I was being fed and cared for at a special table prepared *just for me*, a table prepared by my God. While I was nurtured and strengthened, the cancer cells had nothing. I ended the meditation almost laughing.

The generosity of God does not stop with me. God makes the same promise of a banquet to every person of faith. There are literally millions of such banquets that have been, are being, and will be prepared all around the world. At each banquet only one person will be the guest of honor; your personal banquet will be served to you in the presence of your personal enemies. Such is the prolific generosity of our God.

Use Divine Reading (page 29), Imaginative Prayer (page 44), or both as you reflect upon the generosity of God.

GRATITUDE FOR OUR GENEROUS GOD

O God, it is right for us to
praise you in Zion
and keep our promises to you,
because you answer prayers. . . .

People all over the world
and across the distant seas
trust in you.
You set the mountains in place by
your strength,
showing your mighty power.
You calm the roar of the seas
and the noise of the waves;
you calm the uproar of the
peoples.
The whole world stands in awe
of the great things that you have
done.
Your deeds bring shouts of joy
from one end of the earth to the
other.

You show your care for the land by
sending rain;
you make it rich and fertile.

You fill the streams with water;
you provide the earth with crops.
This is how you do it:
you send abundant rain on the
plowed fields
and soak them with water;
you soften the soil with showers
and cause the young plants to
grow.
What a rich harvest your goodness
provides!
Wherever you go there is plenty.
The pastures are filled with flocks;
the hillsides are full of joy.
The fields are covered with sheep;
the valleys are full of wheat.
Everything shouts and sings
for joy.

—PSALMS 65:1–2, 5–13

Where is God now? At the outset of this journey, that question jarred me to my core. I have rediscovered once again what has always been true: Beyond generous, our God is also trustworthy. Long before I was even born, God promised I would have each day what I needed for that day. Even before there was such a thing as medical science, God in Christ had made available the gift of divine love which, when embraced, promised to carry me beyond the death of my body.

The eruption of feelings after my diagnosis caused me to doubt those promises. The promises were no less true; my faith was less sure. God does not change in the midst of the crises we face throughout our lives; rather, God consistently, relentlessly comes, loving us, unwilling to let anything that happens separate us from the love of our creator.

The God who comes to us is a trustworthy God; promises made are promises kept. They are often not kept in the way we anticipate, but better than we can imagine. They are often not kept on our timetable, but on a better timetable than we propose.

I found that as I put my trust more and more fully in the promises of my creator, I also experienced more and more of the joy in life. It is the deep joy about which Jesus so often spoke, and quite different from happiness, which is too often dependent on what *happens* in our lives. (The two words themselves come from the Middle English word *happenen*, literally "lucky; fortunate"—if good things happen we are happy.) In contrast, joy comes not from what happens to us, good or bad, but from trusting God.

In *Lazarus Laughed*, playwright Eugene O'Neill imagines Lazarus after Jesus has raised him from death. The resurrected Lazarus now knows death to be no more than illusion, and God's promises to be true. With the confidence that insight brings, Lazarus is afraid of nothing and O'Neill pictures him as having a case of the divine giggles. Lazarus finds joy and brings laughter into every situation.

In the final act, Lazarus has again died, this time put to death at the order of Caligula, emperor of Rome. Caligula, in the process of going mad, has a desperate change of heart and cries, "Lazarus! Forgive me! Help me! Fear kills me! Save me from death!" The play closes with the voice of Lazarus coming from beyond the stage laughing and saying, "Fear not, Caligula! There is no death!"

Today, I have never felt more loved by God nor more confident in the promises and the presence of the God who in coming gave me life. I began this book saying I am surviving cancer, and I am a survivor. However, I do not know that I am cured and for me that is no longer really the issue. I trust a wildly, wonderfully generous God who faithfully comes, giving me joy.

Repeated meditation on the same verse can help draw us toward the
attitudes that will best serve us. The challenge to be thankful in all things
is a difficult yet life-giving challenge. Focus on the health challenge in
your own life or the life of your loved one. Use Divine Reading
(page 29) to meditate on these words.

GUIDELINES FOR HAPPINESS

Be joyful always, pray at all times, be thankful in all circum-
stances. This is what God wants from you in your life in union with
Christ Jesus.

—1 THESSALONIANS 5:16–18

Use Divine Reading (page 29) to explore this prayer.

A PRAYER OF THANKSGIVING

Give thanks to the LORD,
       because he is good,
       and his love is eternal.
Let the people of Israel say,
       "His love is eternal."
Let the priests of God say,
       "His love is eternal."
Let all who worship him say,
       "His love is eternal."
In my distress I called to the LORD;
       he answered me and set me
          free.
The LORD is with me, I will not be
          afraid;
       what can anyone do to me?
It is the LORD who helps me,
       and I will see my enemies defeated.
It is better to trust in the LORD
       than to depend on people. . . .

You are my God, and I give you
          thanks;
       I will proclaim your greatness.

Give thanks to the LORD, because
he is good,
and his love is eternal.

—PSALMS 118:1–8, 28–29

REFLECTIONS

Use Divine Reading (page 29), Imaginative Prayer (page 44), or both to affirm God's faithfulness to you.

GOD'S FAITHFULNESS

I waited patiently for the
LORD's help;
then he listened to me and
heard my cry.
He pulled me out of a dangerous
pit,
out of the deadly quicksand.
He set me safely on a rock
and made me secure.
He taught me to sing a new song,
a song of praise to our God.
Many who see this will take
warning
and will put their trust in the
LORD.

—PSALMS 40:1–3

Observe the playfulness and satisfaction described in this passage. What would happen if the joyful generosity of God were withdrawn from creation? Use Divine Reading (page 29), Imaginative Prayer (page 44), or both to let these images play in your mind.

A GIVING GOD

LORD, you have made so many
                things!
                How wisely you made them all!
                The earth is filled with your
                creatures.
There is the ocean, large and wide,
                where countless creatures live,
                large and small alike.
The ships sail on it, and in it plays
                Leviathan,
                that sea monster which you
                made.

All of them depend on you
                to give them food when they
                need it.
You give it to them, and they eat it;
                you provide food, and they are
                satisfied.
When you turn away, they are
                afraid;
                when you take away your
                breath, they die

and go back to the dust from
which they came.
But when you give them breath,
they are created;
you give new life to the earth.

—PSALMS 104:24—30

REFLECTIONS

Use Divine Reading (page 29), Imaginative Prayer (page 44), or both
to bring Paul's words alive in your heart.

A Response to God's Help

Let us give thanks to the God and Father of our LORD Jesus Christ, the merciful Father, the God from whom all help comes! He helps us in all our troubles, so that we are able to help others who have all kinds of troubles using the same help that we ourselves have received from God. Just as we have a share in Christ's many sufferings, so also through Christ we share in God's great help.

—2 CORINTHIANS 1:3–5

Use Divine Reading (page 29), Imaginative Prayer (page 44), or both in a celebration of the love God has for you.

GOD'S LOVE

Praise the LORD, my soul!
All my being, praise his
holy name!
Praise the LORD, my soul,
and do not forget how kind
he is.
He forgives all my sins
and heals all my diseases.
He keeps me from the grave
and blesses me with love and
mercy. . . .

As high as the sky is above the
earth,
so great is his love for those who
honor him.
As far as the east is from the west,
so far does he remove our sins
from us.
As a father is kind to his children,
so the LORD is kind to those who
honor him.
He knows what we are made of;
he remembers that we are dust.

As for us, our life is like grass.
We grow and flourish like a wild
flower;
then the wind blows on it, and it
is gone—
no one sees it again.
But for those who honor the LORD,
his love lasts forever,
and his goodness endures for all
generations.

—PSALMS 103:1–4, 11–17

REFLECTIONS

This final meditation I offer as a gift to you. I have found Psalm 131 to be one of the most comforting and encouraging there is. I return to it often when I begin to worry about my life as if I were the one in total control. As you meditate on this passage, focus on the tenderness of God's desire to nourish and comfort you. Picture the security of a baby drawn close to the breast of her mother. Use Divine Reading (page 29) to let the words soothe your heart and mind. Since you are a part of the New Israel, the church, substitute your own name for the word "Israel" at the end of the Psalm and let this be a personal invitation to you to constantly renew your trust in God. May God bless you on your journey.

Pray.

A PRAYER OF HUMBLE TRUST

LORD, I have given up my
pride
and turned away from my
arrogance.
I am not concerned with great
matters
or with subjects too difficult
for me.
Instead, I am content and at peace.
As a child lies quietly in its
mother's arms,
so my heart is quiet within me.
Israel, trust in the LORD
now and forever!

—PSALMS 131